FOR ORGANS, PIANOS & ELECTRONIC KEYBOARDS

E-Z PLAY® TODAY

87

50 WORSHIP STANDARDS

ISBN 978-1-4234-9295-5

HAL•LEONARD®
CORPORATION

7777 W. BLUEMOUND RD. P.O. BOX 13819 MILWAUKEE, WI 53213

Visit Hal Leonard Online at
www.halleonard.com

CONTENTS

Above All

Registration 1
Rhythm: Ballad or 8-Beat

Words and Music by Paul Baloche
and Lenny LeBlanc

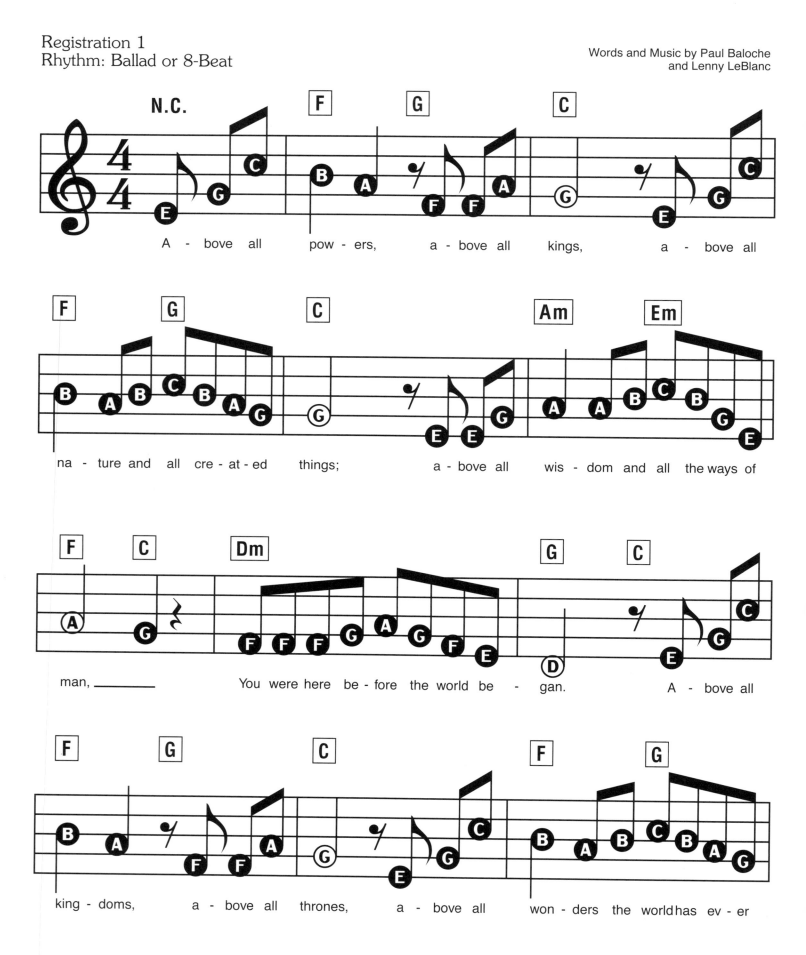

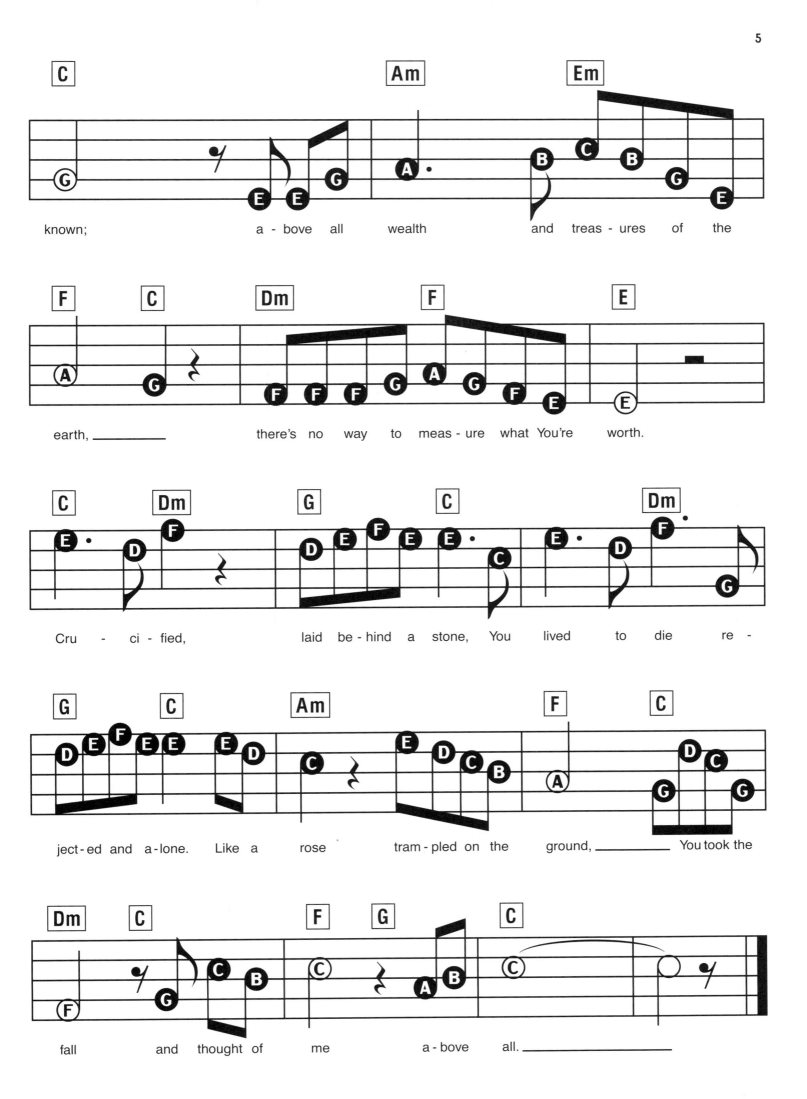

Agnus Dei

Registration 1
Rhythm: Ballad or 8-Beat

Words and Music by
Michael W. Smith

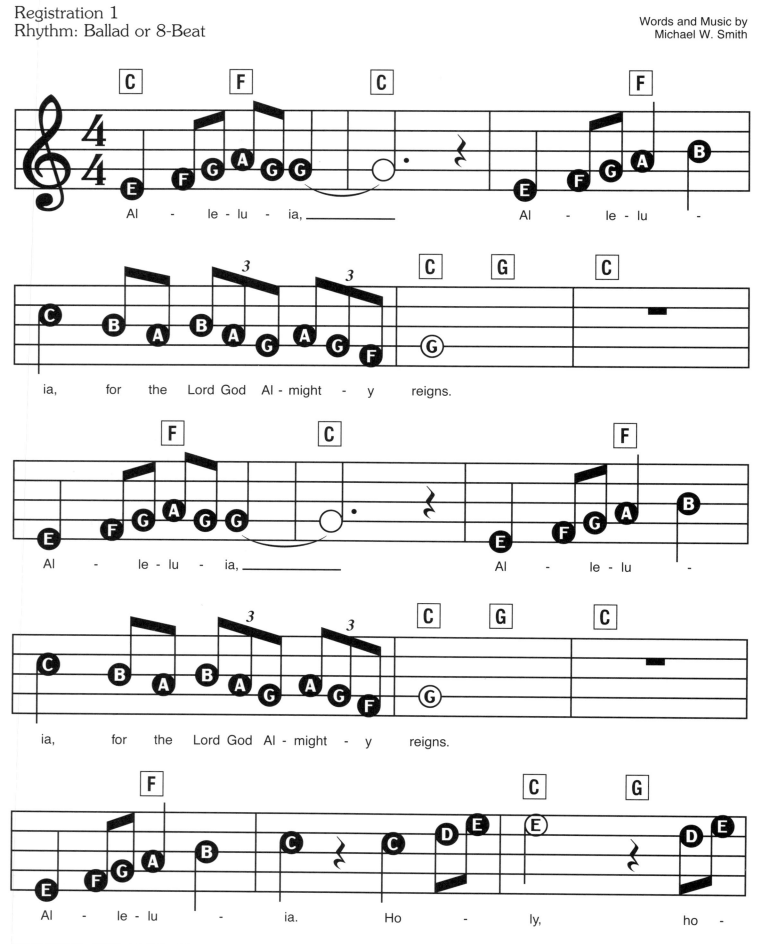

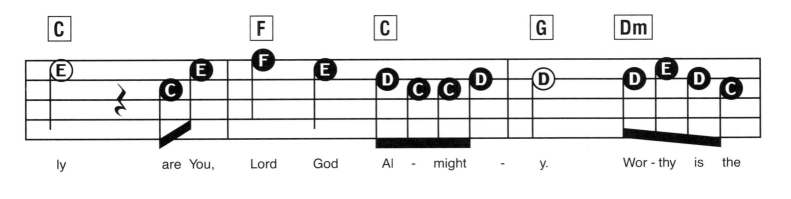

ly   are You,   Lord God   Al - might - y.   Wor - thy is the

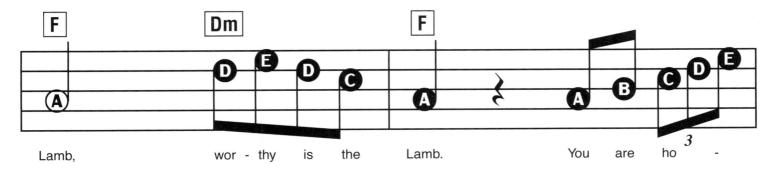

Lamb,   wor - thy is the   Lamb.   You   are   ho -

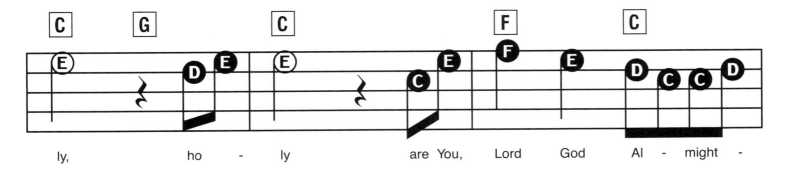

ly,   ho - ly   are You,   Lord God   Al - might -

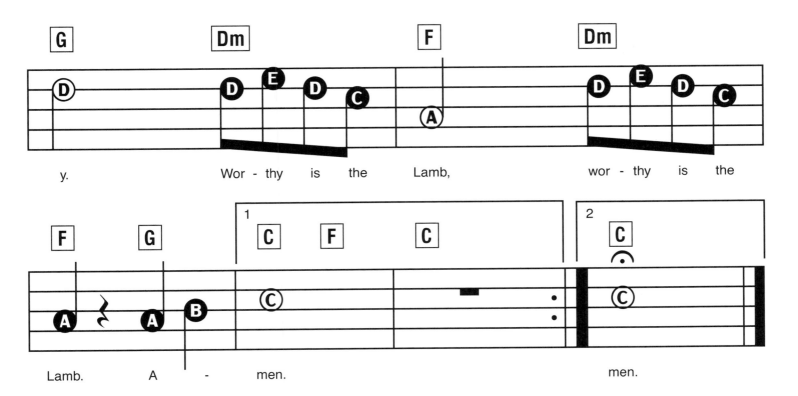

y.   Wor - thy is the   Lamb,   wor - thy is the

Lamb.   A - men.   men.

Ancient Words

Registration 1
Rhythm: None

Words and Music by
Lynn DeShazo

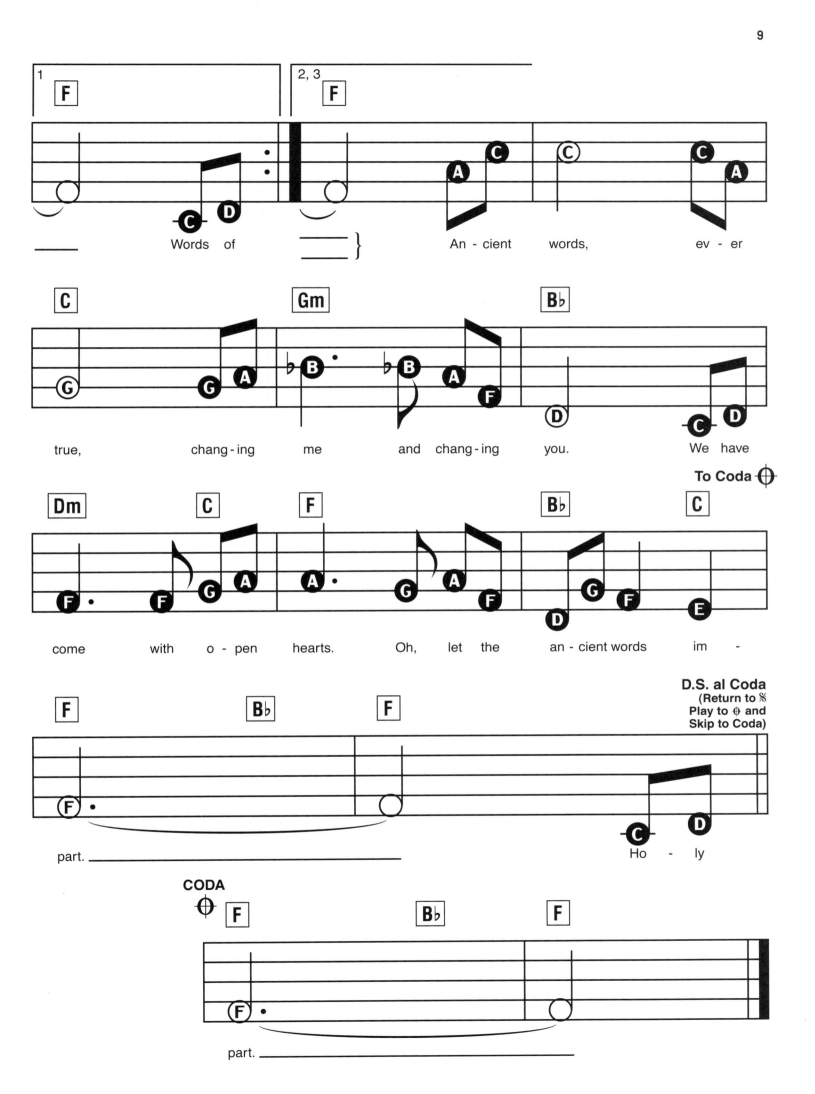

Awesome God

Registration 7
Rhythm: 16-Beat or Pop

Words and Music by
Rich Mullins

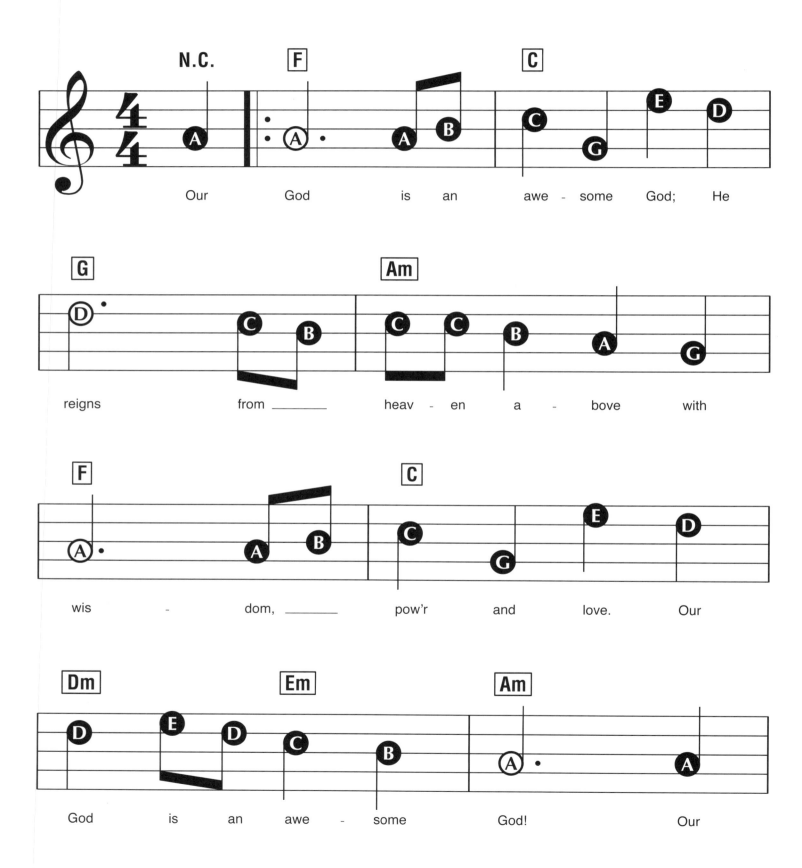

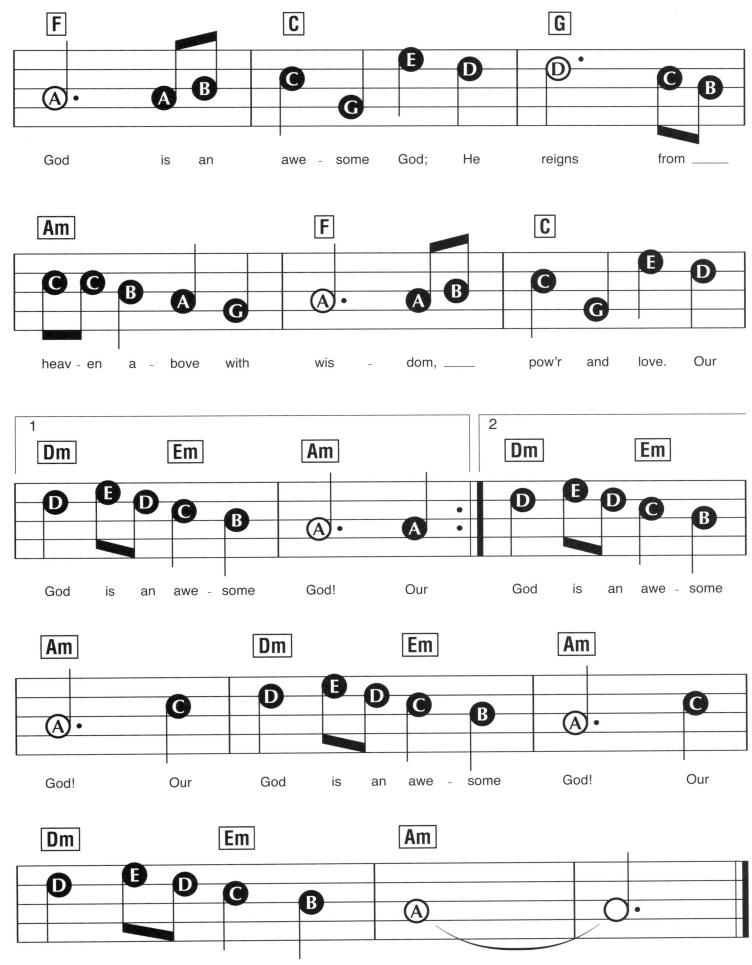

Awesome in This Place

Registration 8
Rhythm: Ballad or 8-Beat

Words and Music by
David Billington

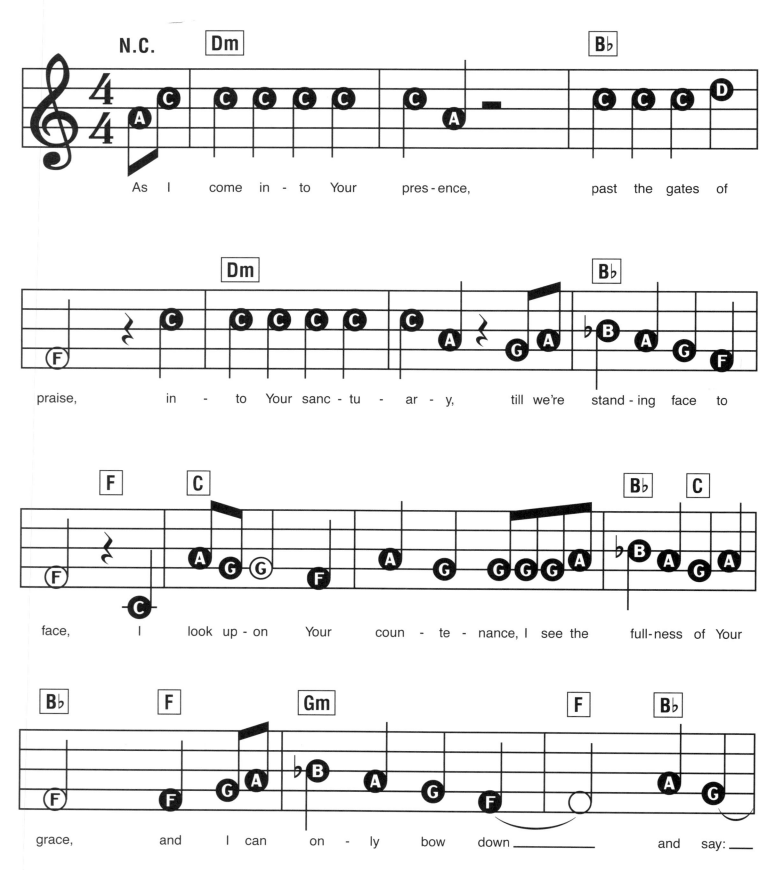

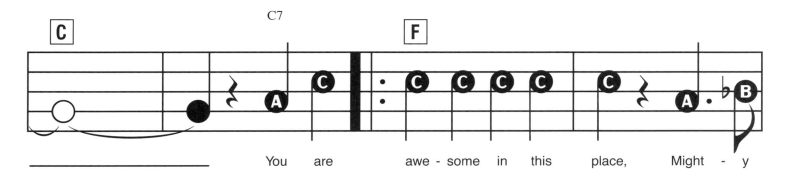

You are awe - some in this place, Might - y

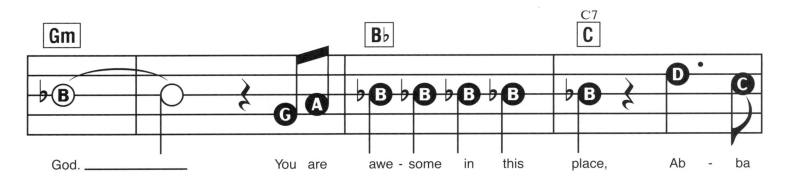

God. _____ You are awe - some in this place, Ab - ba

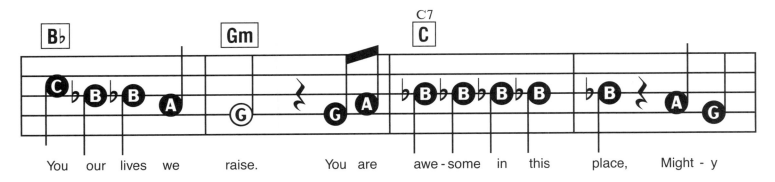

Fa - ther. _____ You are wor - thy of all praise, to

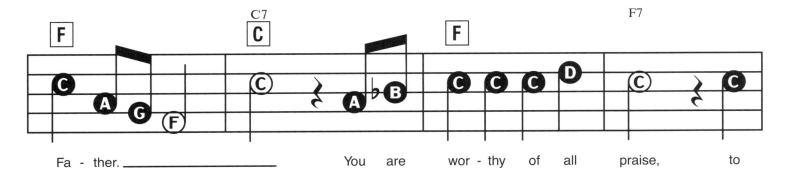

You our lives we raise. You are awe - some in this place, Might - y

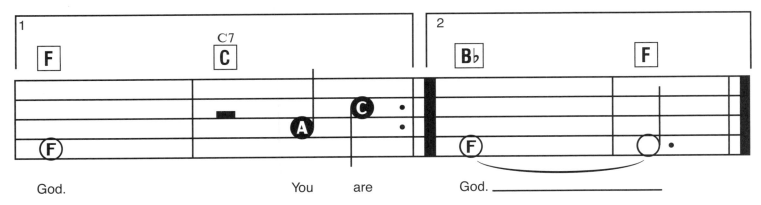

God. You are God. _____

Bless His Holy Name

Registration 2
Rhythm: March

Words and Music by
Andraé Crouch

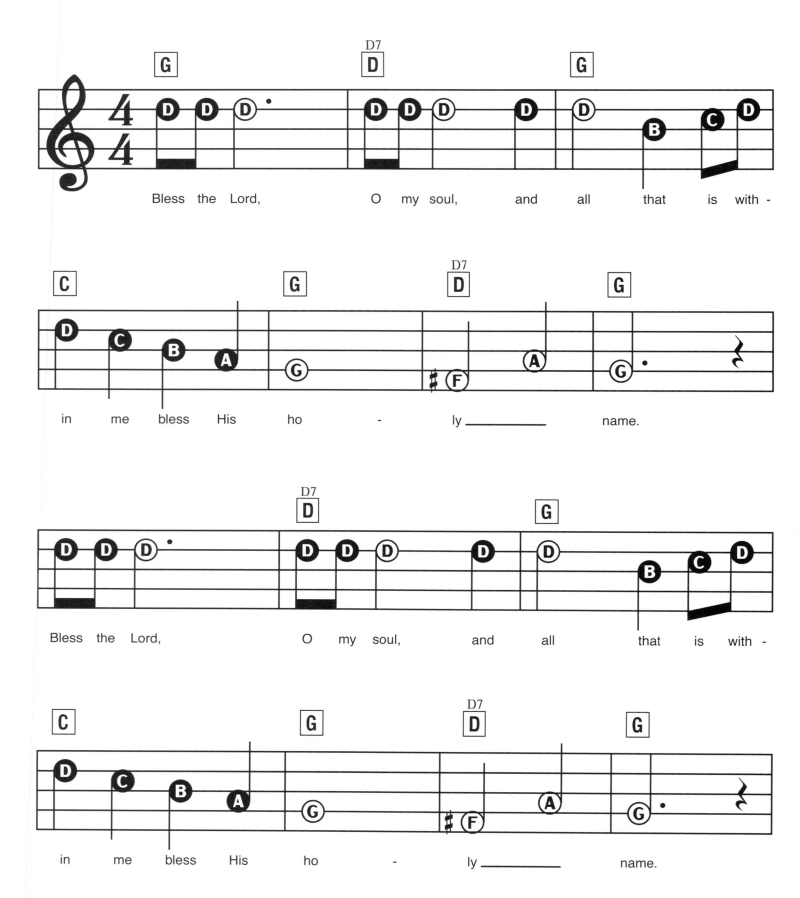

Bless the Lord, O my soul, and all that is with -

in me bless His ho - ly _____ name.

Bless the Lord, O my soul, and all that is with -

in me bless His ho - ly _____ name.

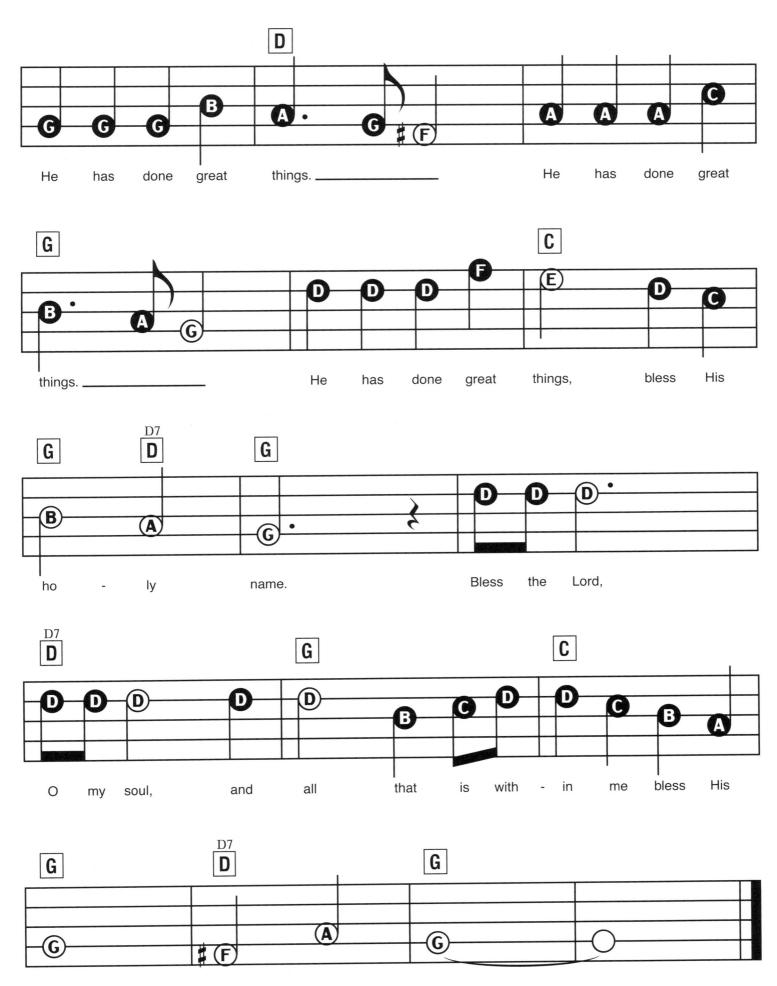

Come Let Us Worship and Bow Down

Registration 1
Rhythm: Ballad

Words and Music by
Dave Doherty

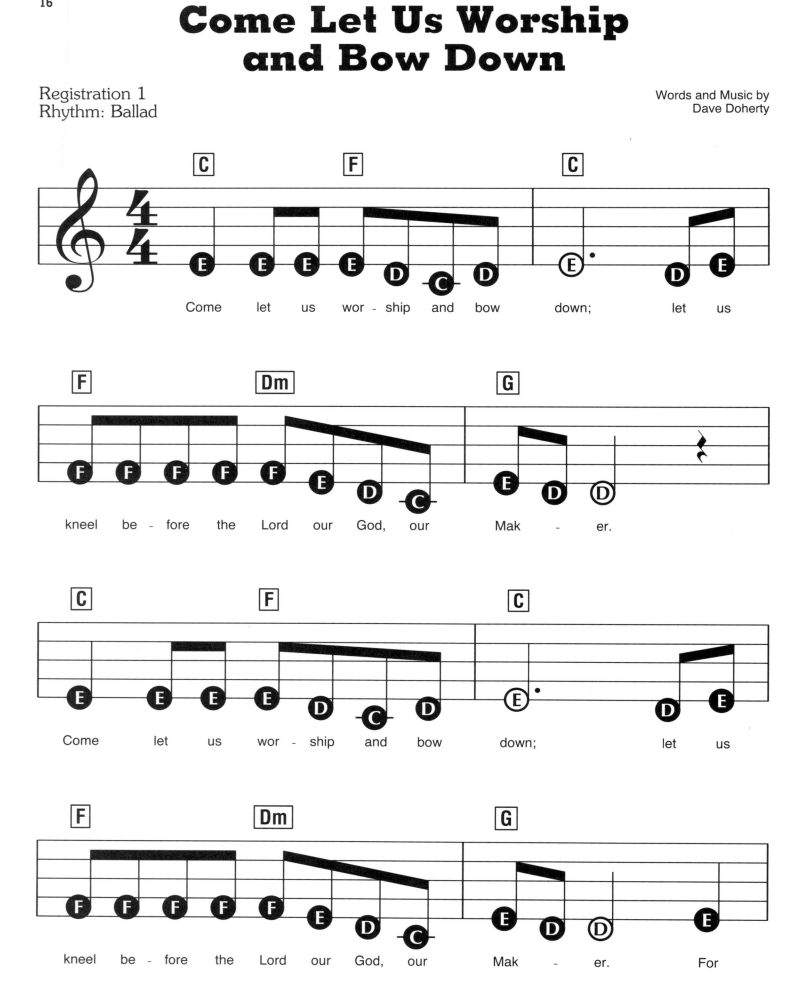

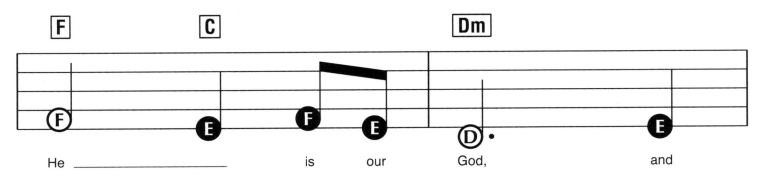

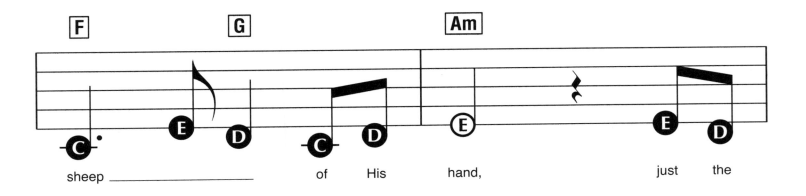

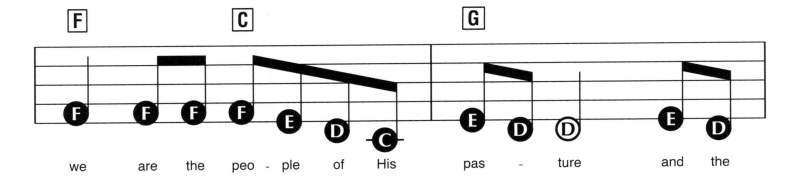

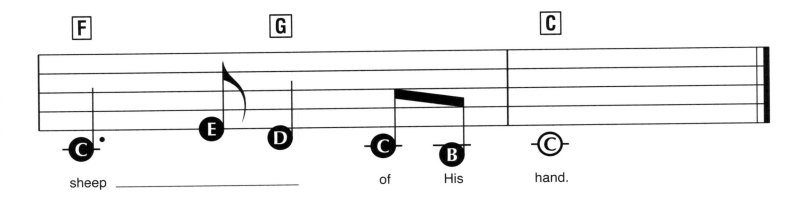

Come, Now Is the Time to Worship

Registration 7
Rhythm: 8-Beat or Rock

Words and Music by
Brian Doerksen

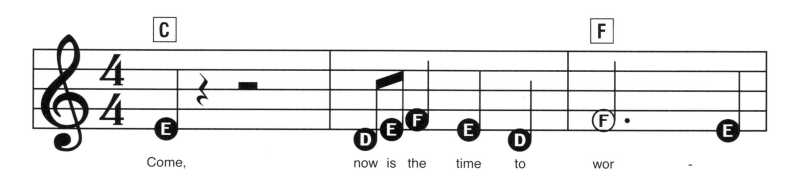

Come, now is the time to wor -

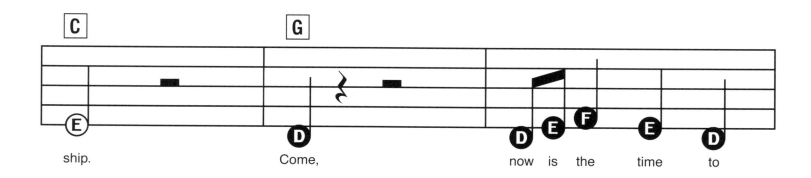

ship. Come, now is the time to

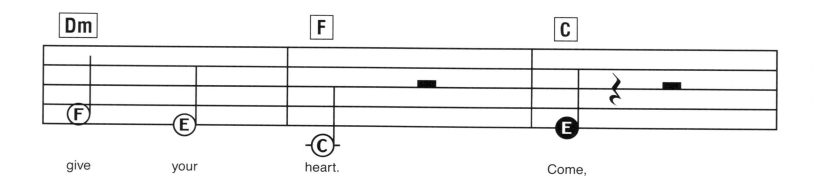

give your heart. Come,

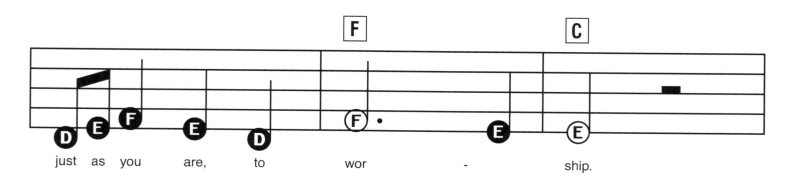

just as you are, to wor - ship.

19

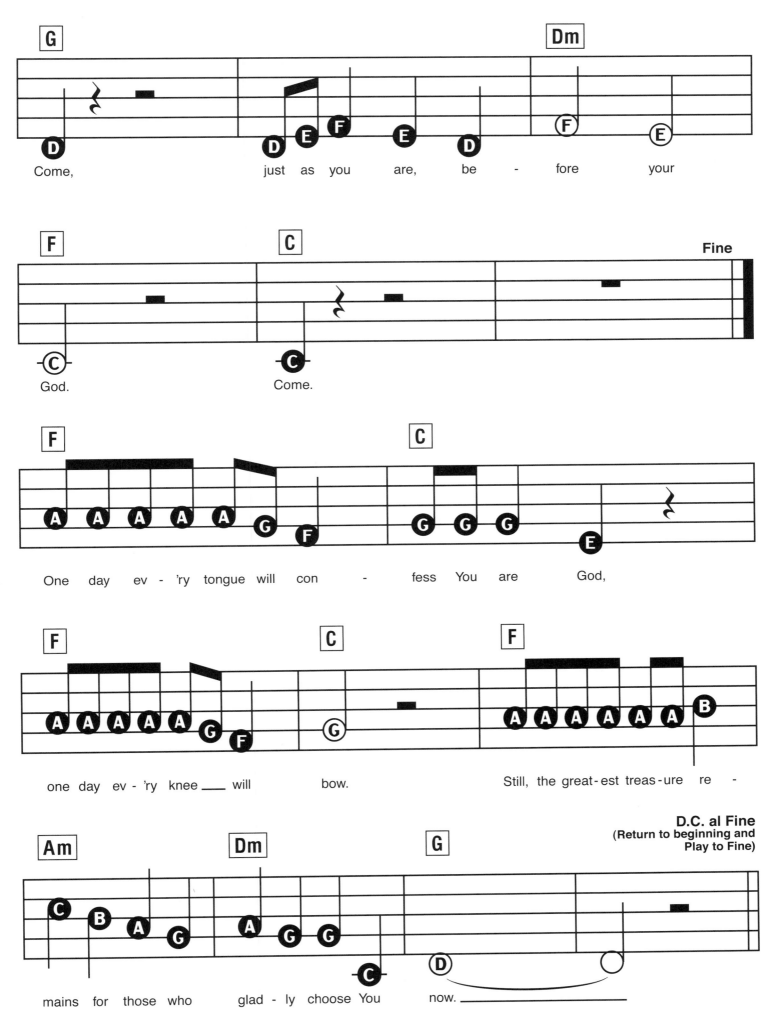

Give Thanks

Registration 1
Rhythm: Ballad

Words and Music by
Henry Smith

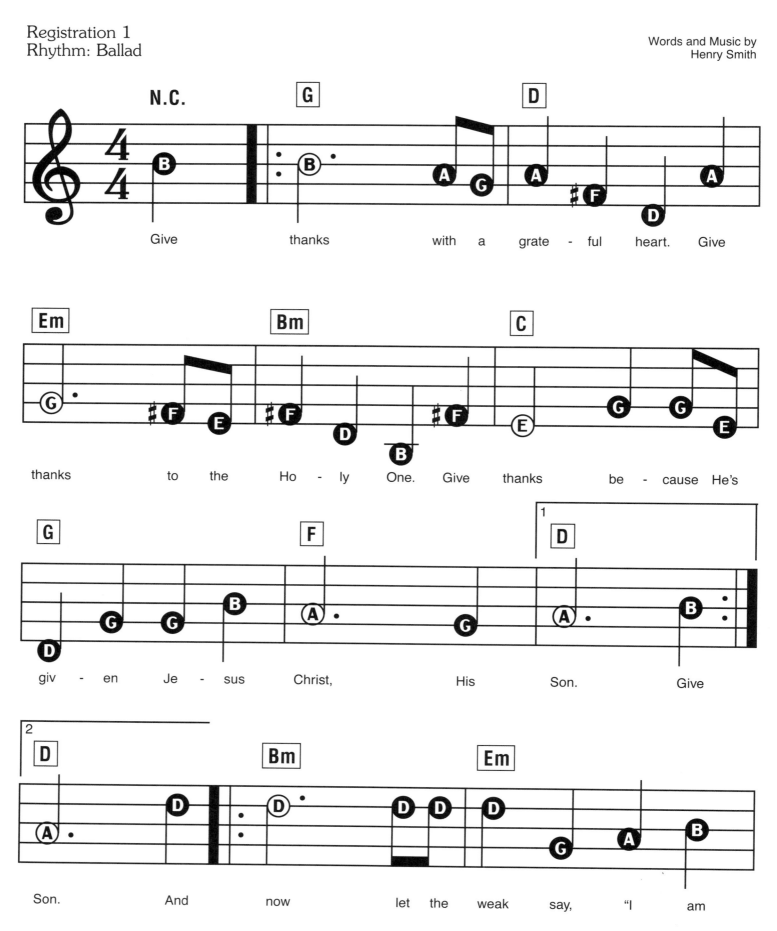

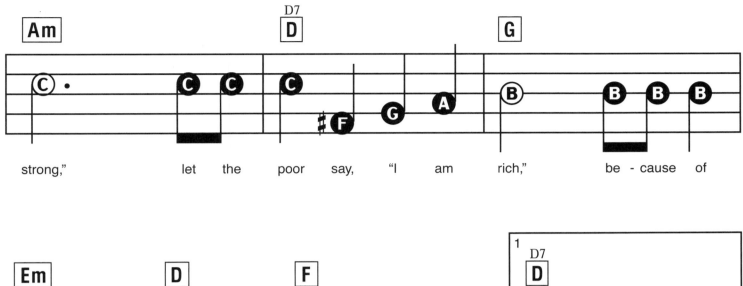

strong,"   let the poor say, "I am rich,"   be - cause of

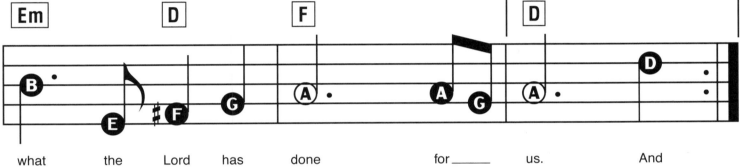

what   the   Lord   has   done   for _____ us.   And

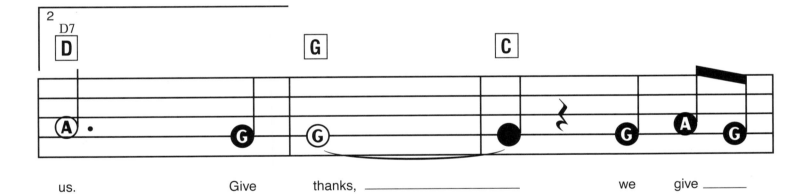

us.   Give   thanks, _____   we   give _____

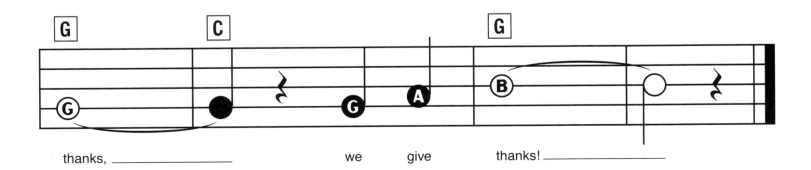

thanks, _____   we   give   thanks! _____

Great Is the Lord

Registration 7
Rhythm: Waltz

Words and Music by Michael W. Smith
and Deborah D. Smith

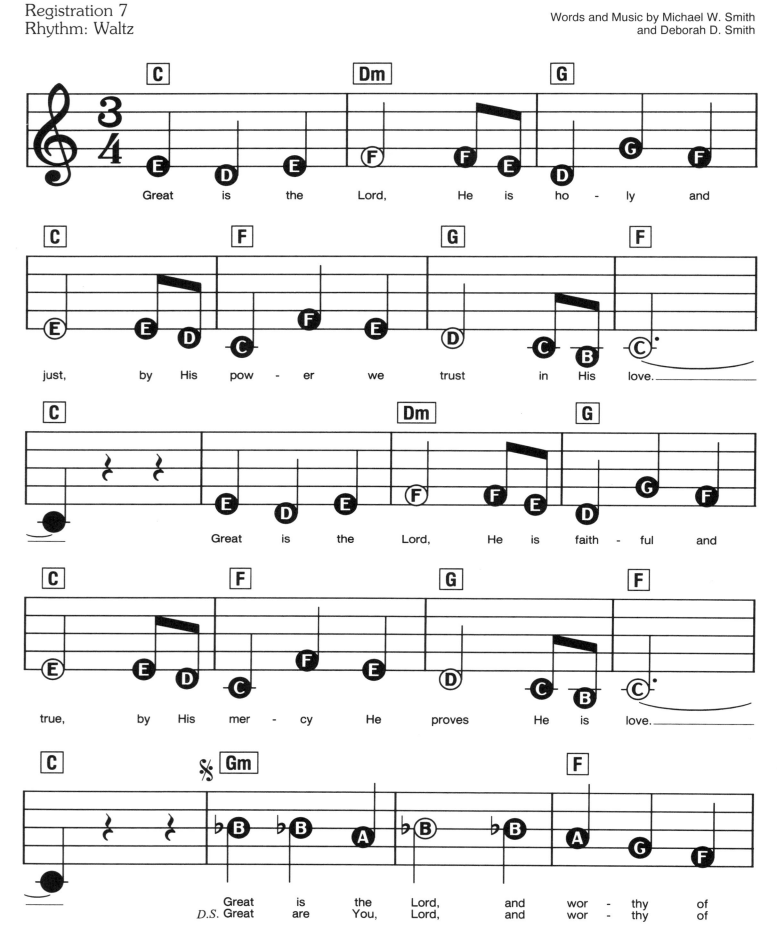

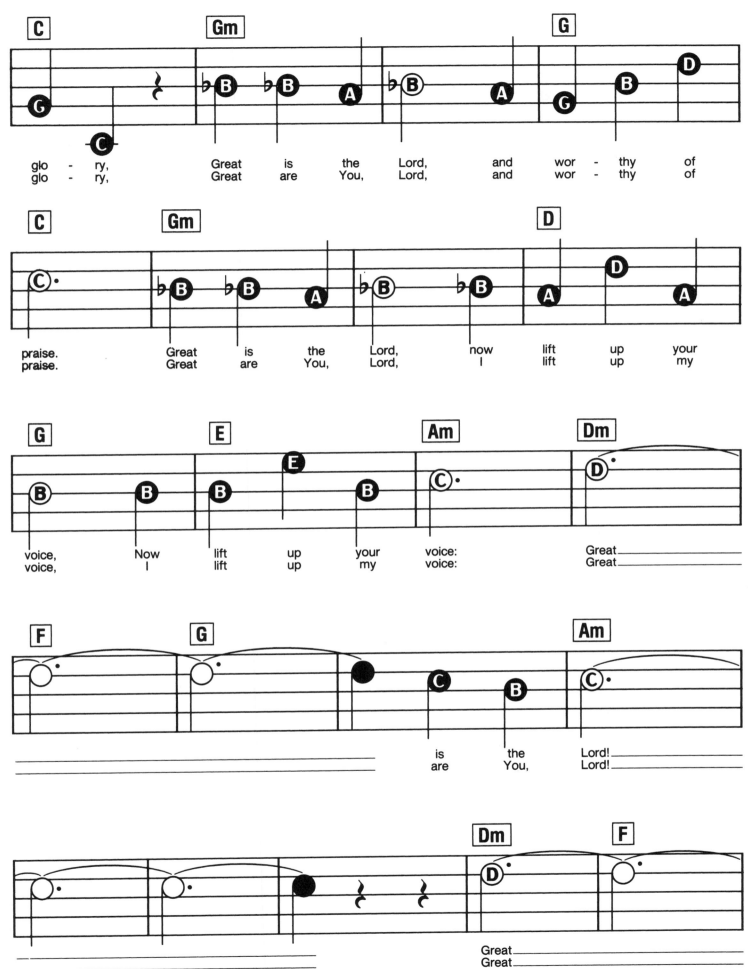

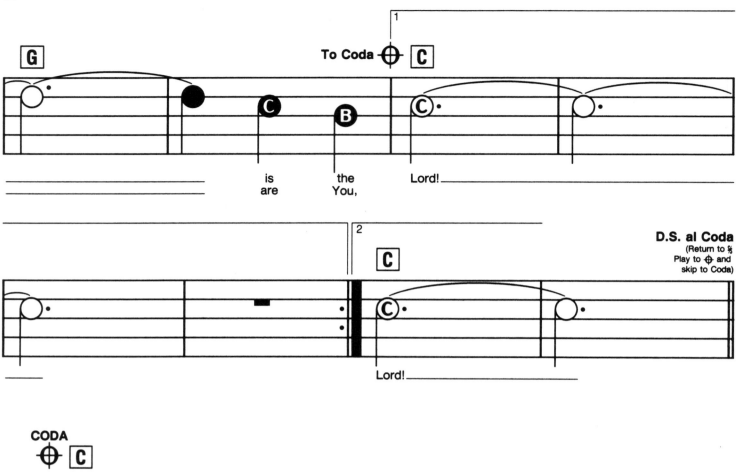

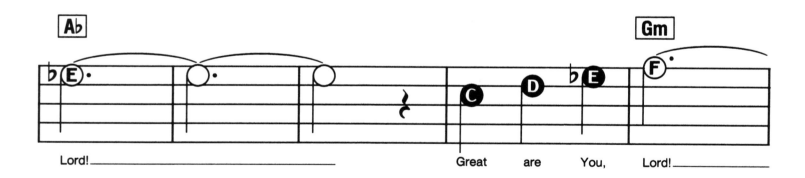

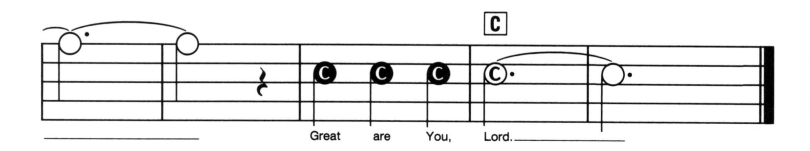

Blessed Be Your Name

Registration 8
Rhythm: 8-Beat or Rock

Words and Music by Matt Redman
and Beth Redman

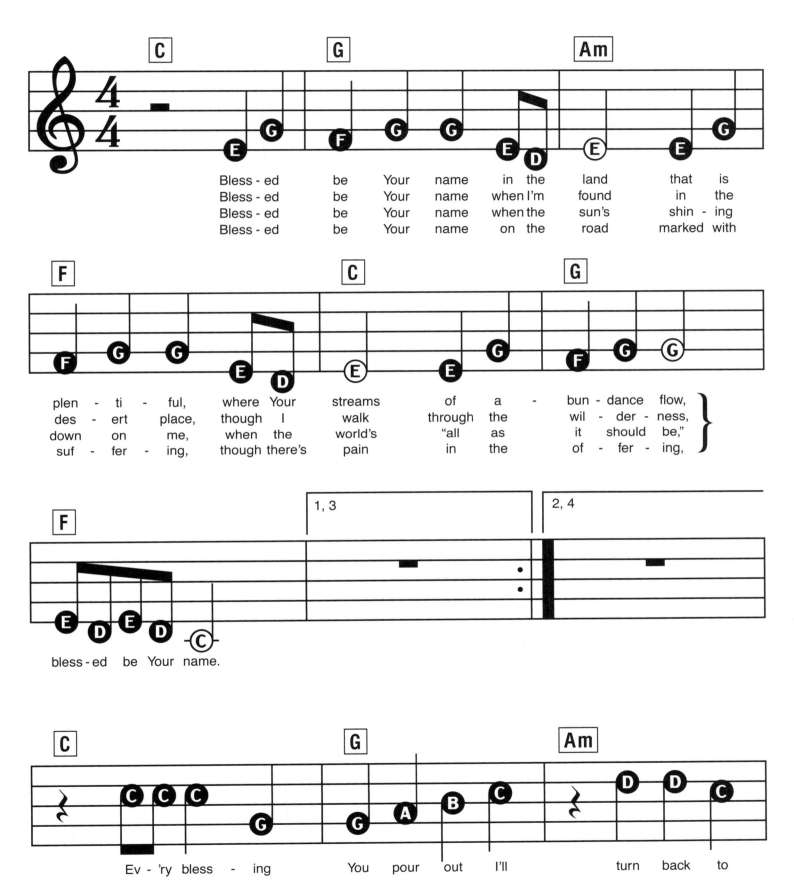

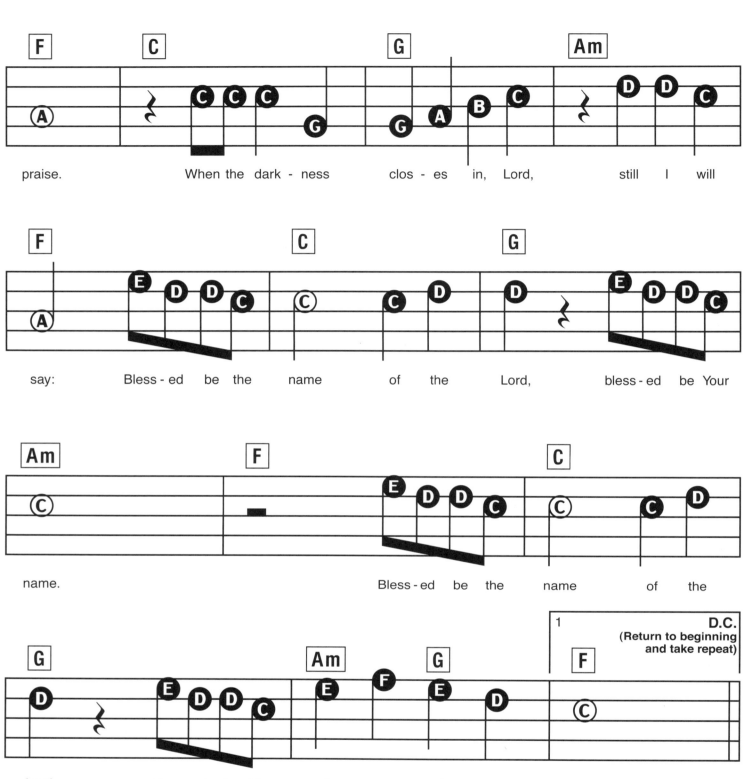

praise.   When the dark - ness clos - es in, Lord,   still I will

say: Bless - ed be the name of the Lord,   bless - ed be Your

name.   Bless - ed be the name of the

Lord,   bless - ed be Your glo - ri - ous name.

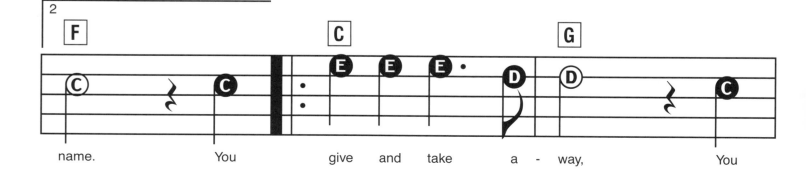

name.   You give and take a - way,   You

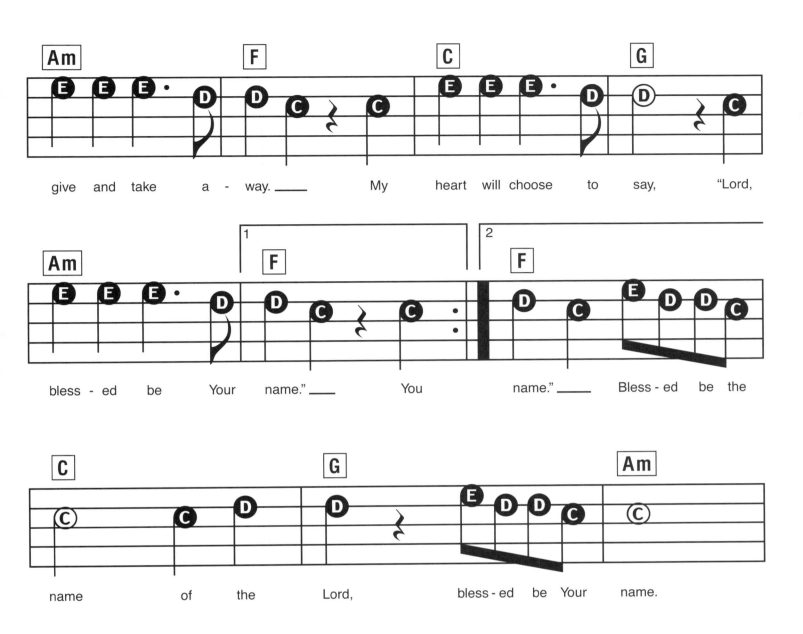

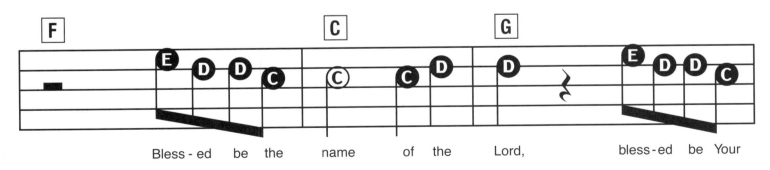

The Heart of Worship

Registration 1
Rhythm: Ballad or 8-Beat

Words and Music by
Matt Redman

When the mu - sic fades, all is stripped a -
King of end - less worth, no one could ex -

way, and I sim - ply come,
press how much You de - serve.

long - ing just to bring some - thing that's of
Though I'm weak and poor, all I have is

worth that will bless Your heart,
Yours, ev - 'ry sin - gle breath.

29

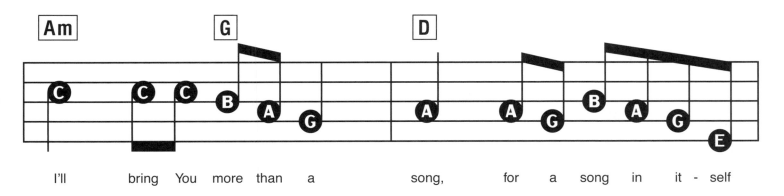

I'll   bring   You   more   than   a   song,   for   a   song   in   it - self

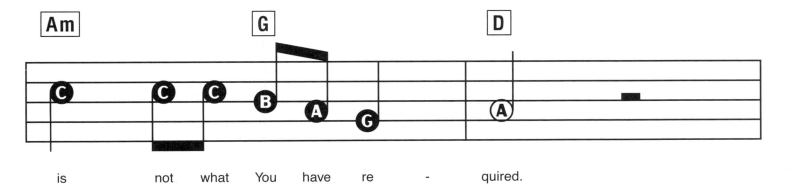

is   not   what   You   have   re   -   quired.

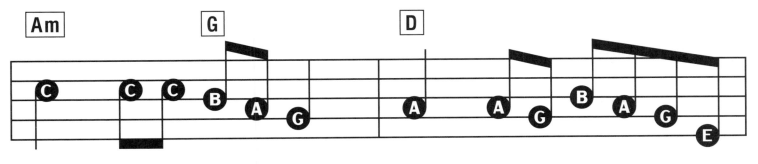

You   search much deep - er   with   -   in,   through the   way   things   ap - pear;

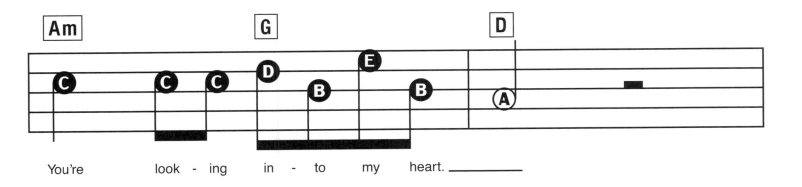

You're   look - ing   in - to   my   heart. _____

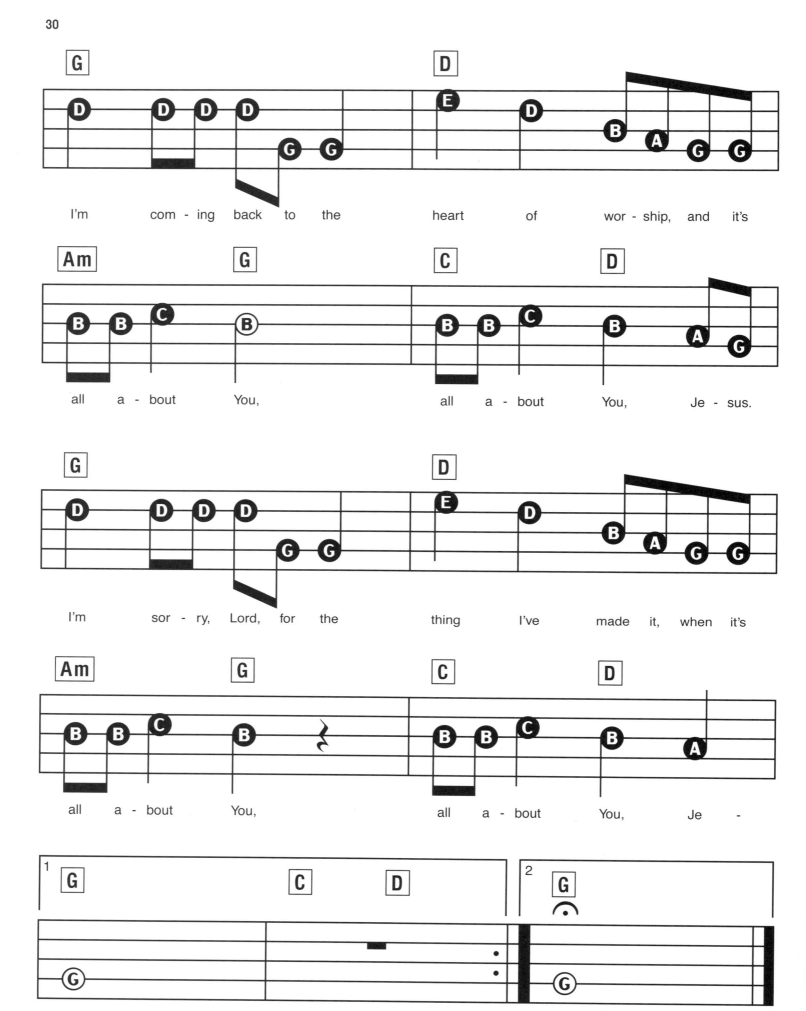

I'm com - ing back to the heart of wor - ship, and it's

all a - bout You, all a - bout You, Je - sus.

I'm sor - ry, Lord, for the thing I've made it, when it's

all a - bout You, all a - bout You, Je -

sus. sus.

He Is Exalted

Registration 2
Rhythm: Waltz

Words and Music by
Twila Paris

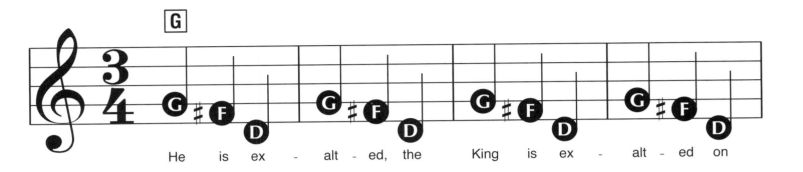

He is ex - alt - ed, the King is ex - alt - ed on

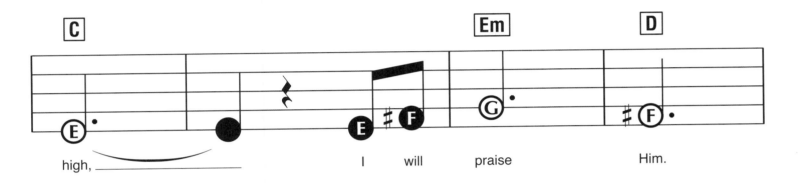

high, _____ I will praise Him.

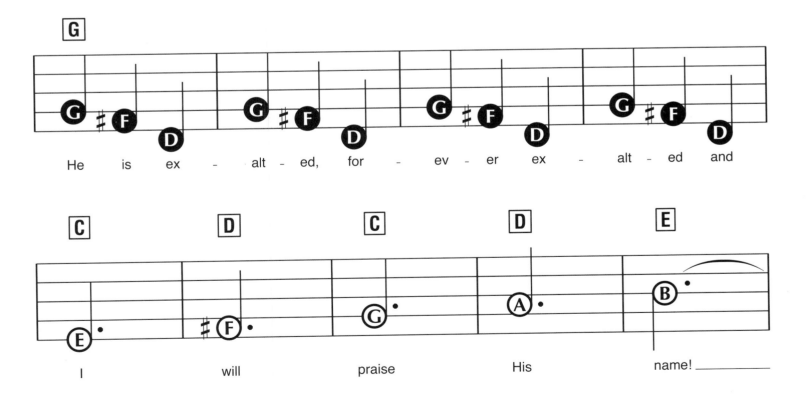

He is ex - alt - ed, for - ev - er ex - alt - ed and

I will praise His name! _____

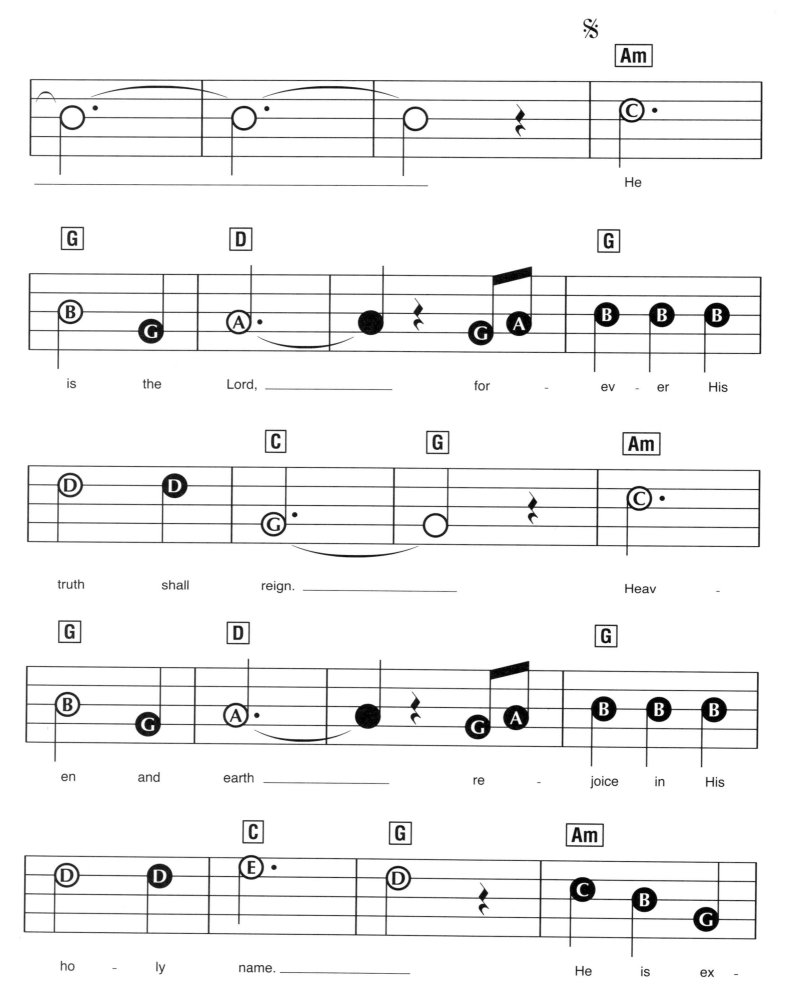

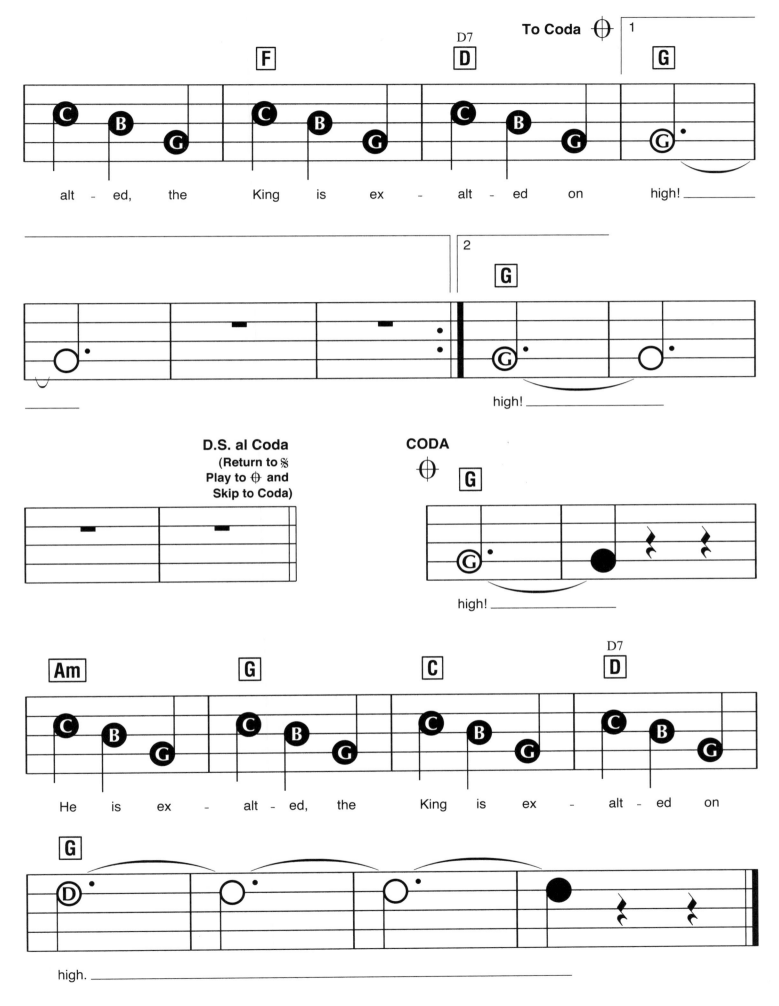

His Name Is Wonderful

Registration 1
Rhythm: Waltz

Words and Music by
Audrey Mieir

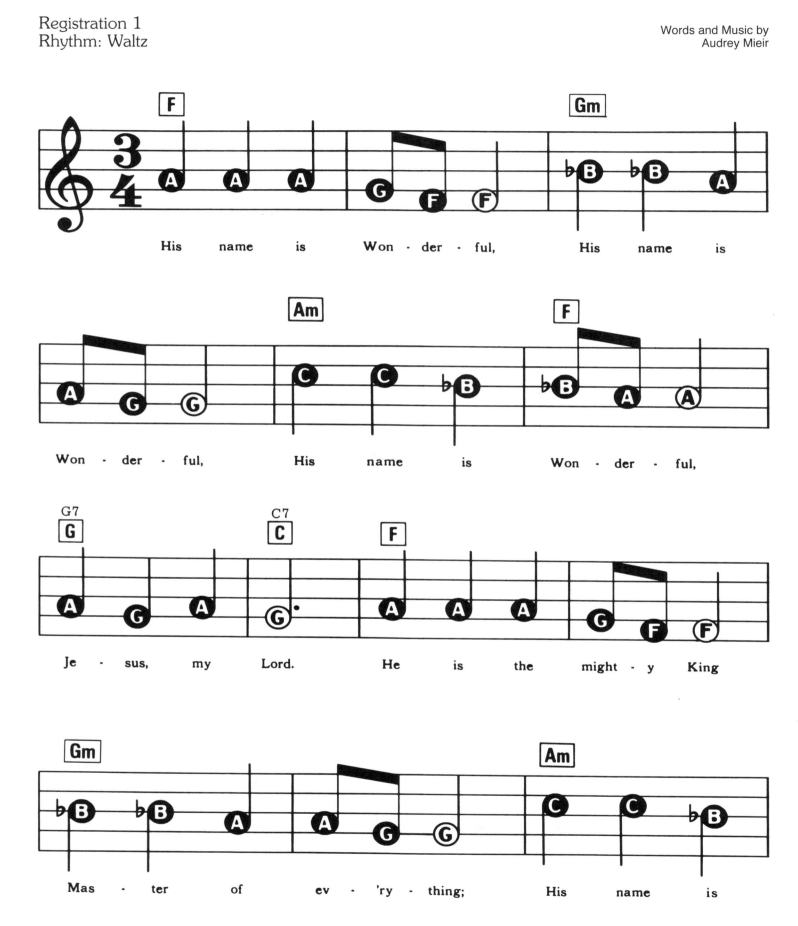

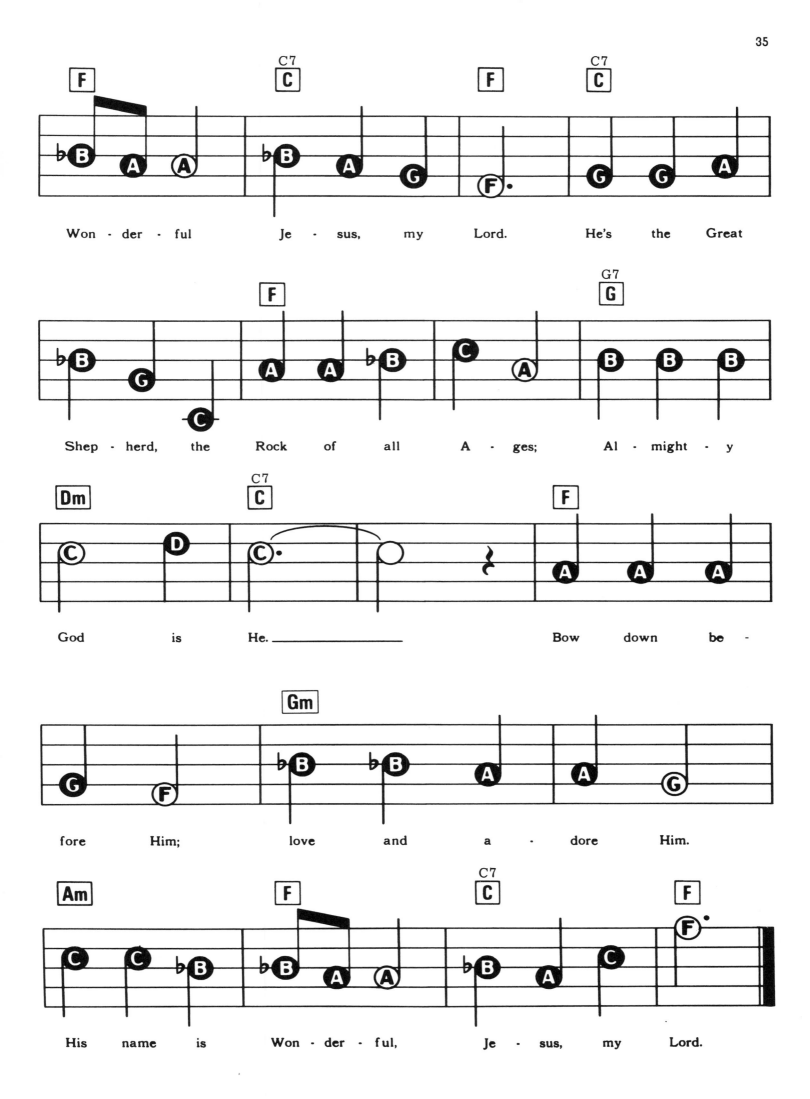

Holy Ground

Registration 3
Rhythm: Ballad or 8-Beat

Words and Music by
Geron Davis

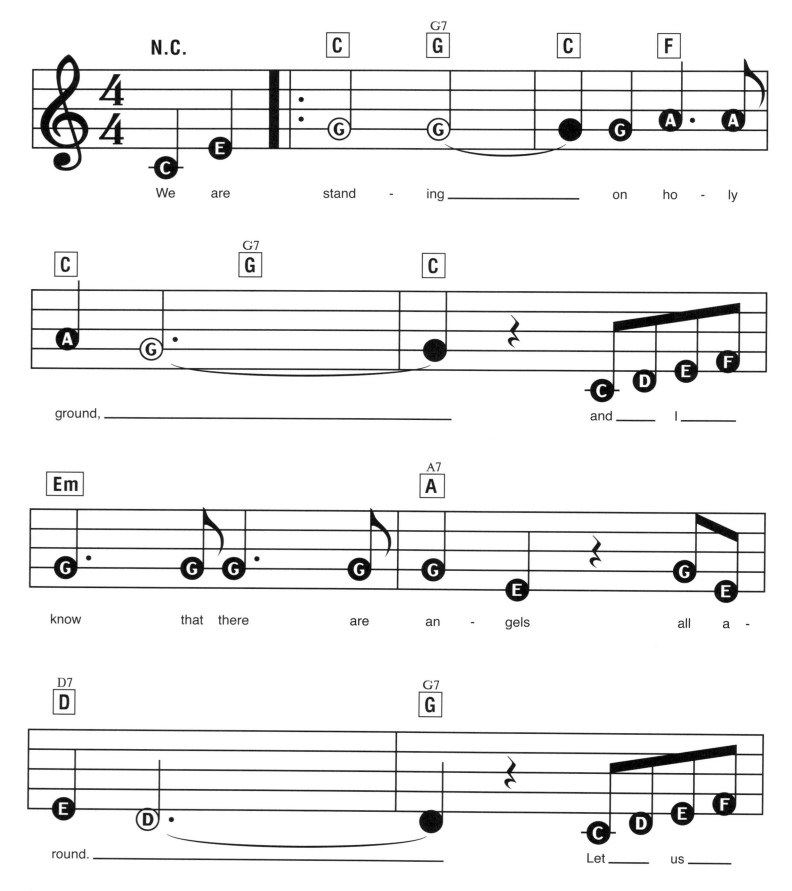

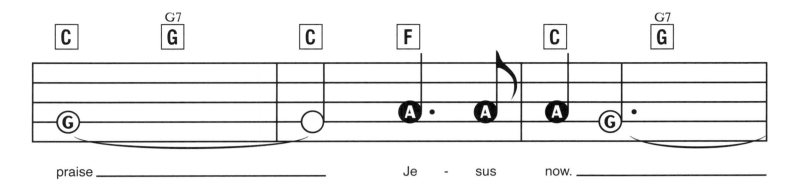

praise _____ Je - sus now. _____

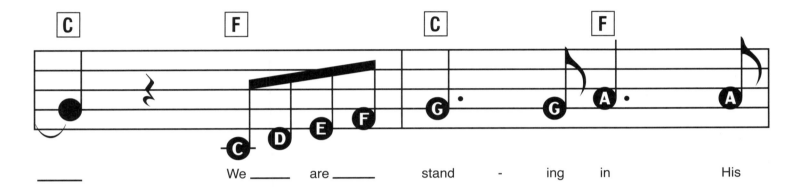

___ We ___ are ___ stand - ing in His

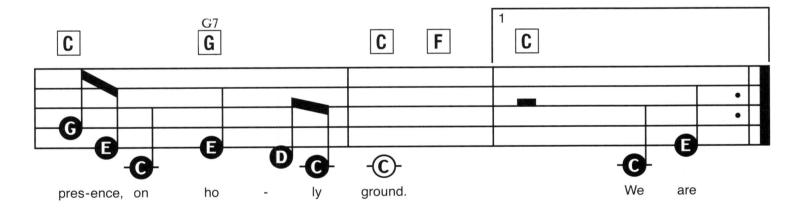

pres-ence, on ho - ly ground. We are

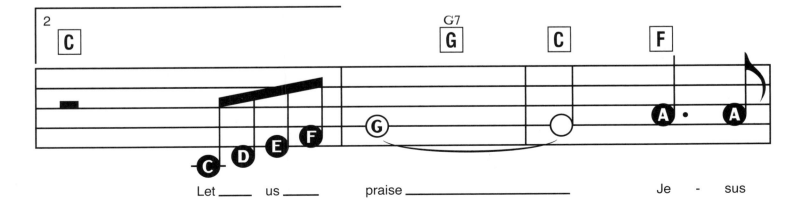

Let ___ us ___ praise _____ Je - sus

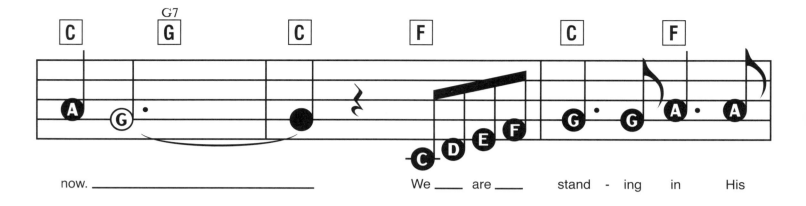

now. _____ We ___ are ___ stand - ing in His

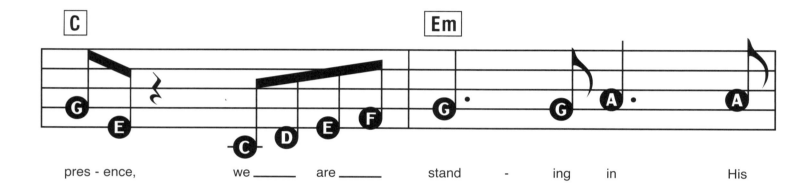

pres - ence, we _____ are _____ stand - ing in His

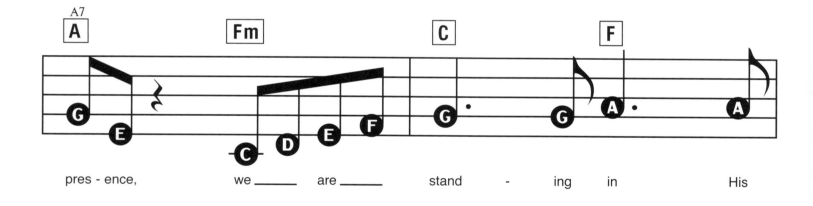

pres - ence, we _____ are _____ stand - ing in His

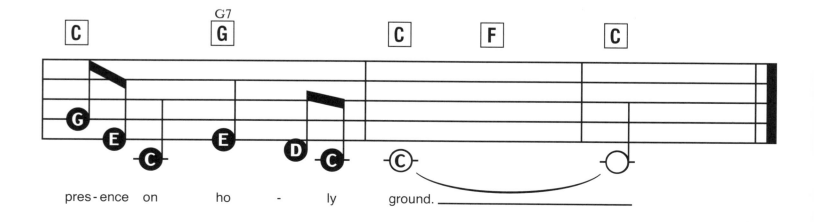

pres - ence on ho - ly ground. _____

Here I Am to Worship

Registration 4
Rhythm: Ballad or 8-Beat

Words and Music by
Tim Hughes

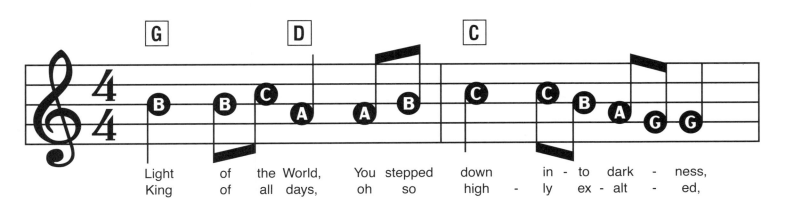

Light of the World, You stepped down in - to dark - ness,
King of all days, oh so high - ly ex - alt - ed,

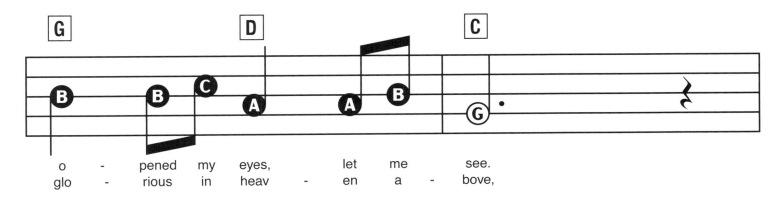

o - pened my eyes, let me see.
glo - rious in heav - en a - bove,

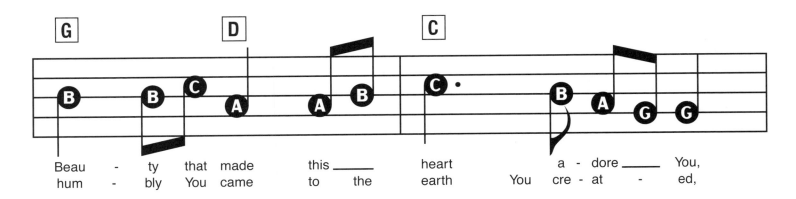

Beau - ty that made this ___ heart a - dore ___ You,
hum - bly You came to the earth You cre - at - ed,

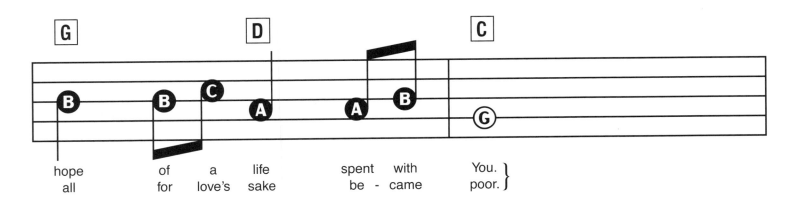

hope of a life spent with You.
all for love's sake be - came poor.

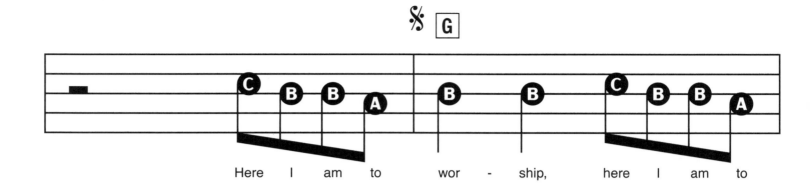

Here I am to wor - ship, here I am to

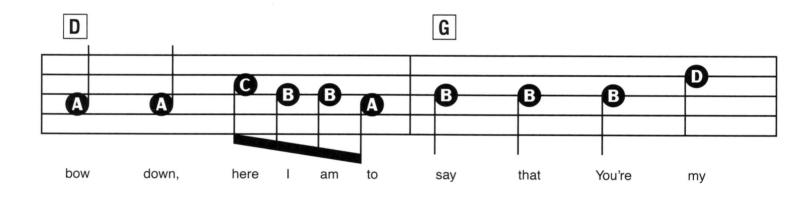

bow down, here I am to say that You're my

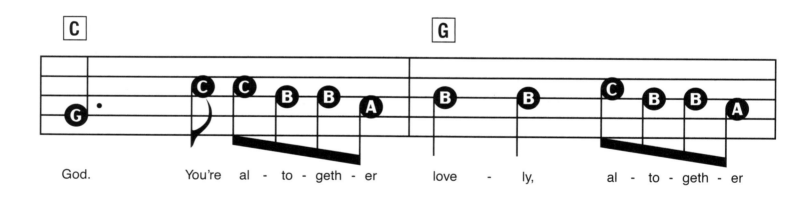

God. You're al - to - geth - er love - ly, al - to - geth - er

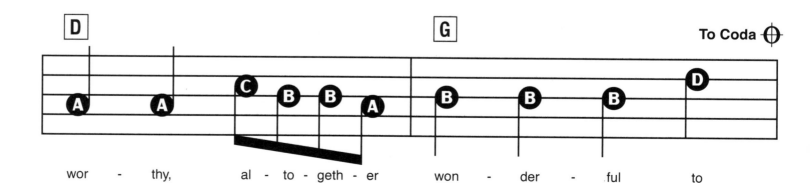

wor - thy, al - to - geth - er won - der - ful to

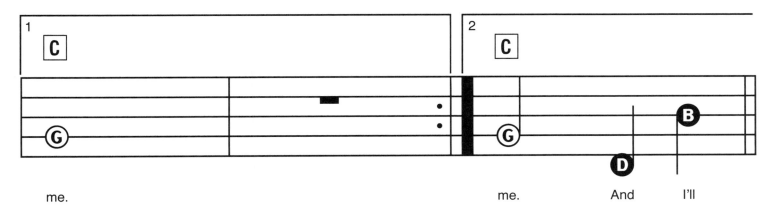

me.　　　　　　　　　　　　　　　　　　　　me.　　And　　I'll

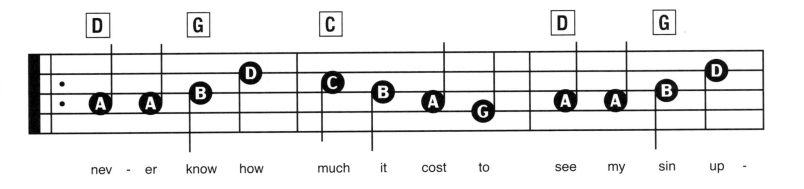

nev - er　know　how　　much　it　cost　to　　see　my　sin　up -

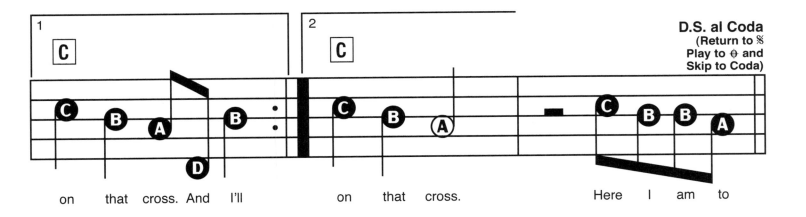

on　that　cross. And　I'll　　on　that　cross.　　Here　I　am　to

D.S. al Coda
(Return to %
Play to ⊕ and
Skip to Coda)

CODA
⊕ [C]　　　　　　　　　　　　　[G]

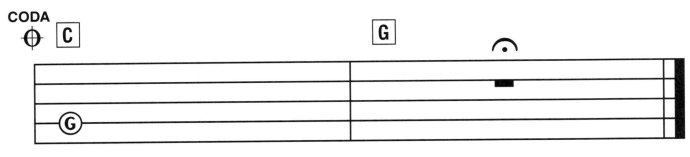

me.

How Deep the Father's Love for Us

Registration 8
Rhythm: Ballad

Words and Music by
Stuart Townend

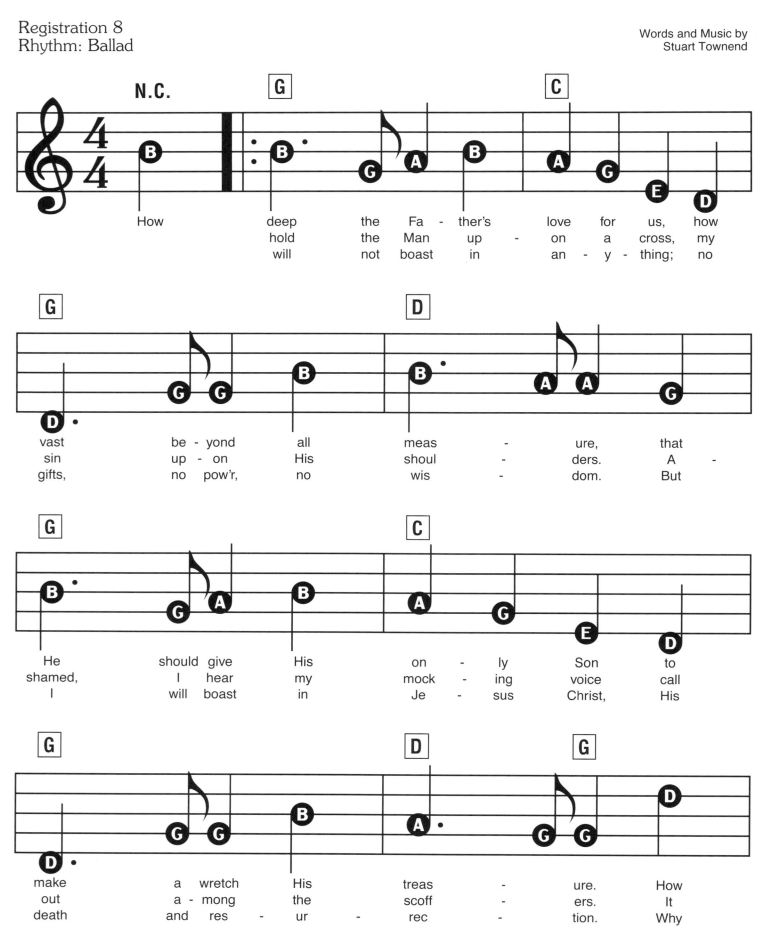

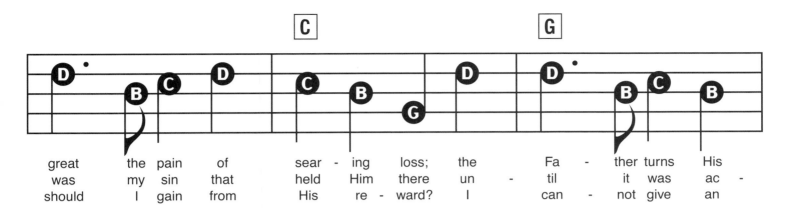

great the pain of sear - ing loss; the Fa - ther turns His
was my sin of that held Him there un - til it was ac -
should I gain from His re - ward? I can - not give an

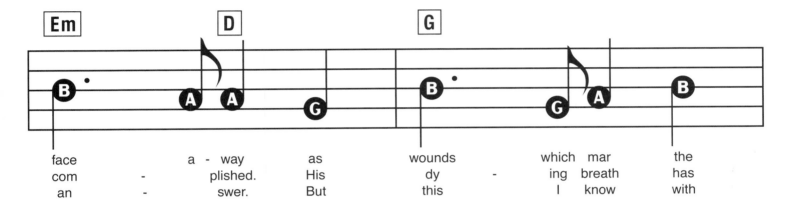

face   a - way as wounds which mar the
com - plished. His dy - ing breath has
an - swer. But this I know with

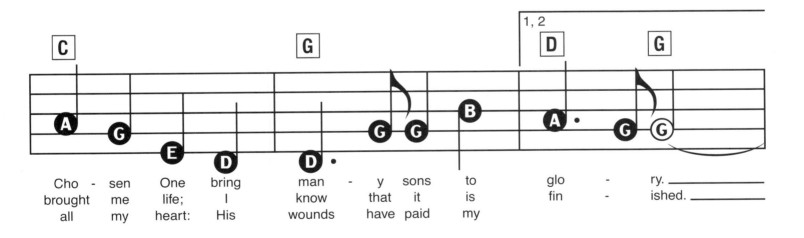

Cho - sen One bring man - y sons to glo - ry. _____
brought me life; I know that it is fin - ished. _____
all my heart: His wounds have paid my

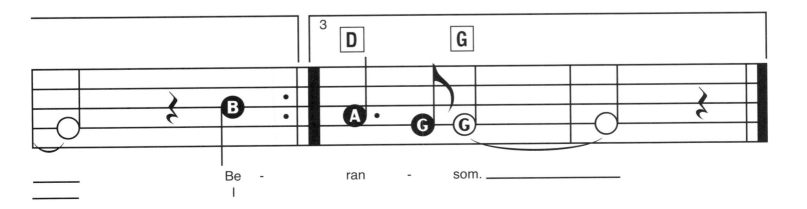

_____ Be - ran - som. _____
    I

How Great Thou Art

Registration 6
Rhythm: Ballad

Words and Music by
Stuart K. Hine

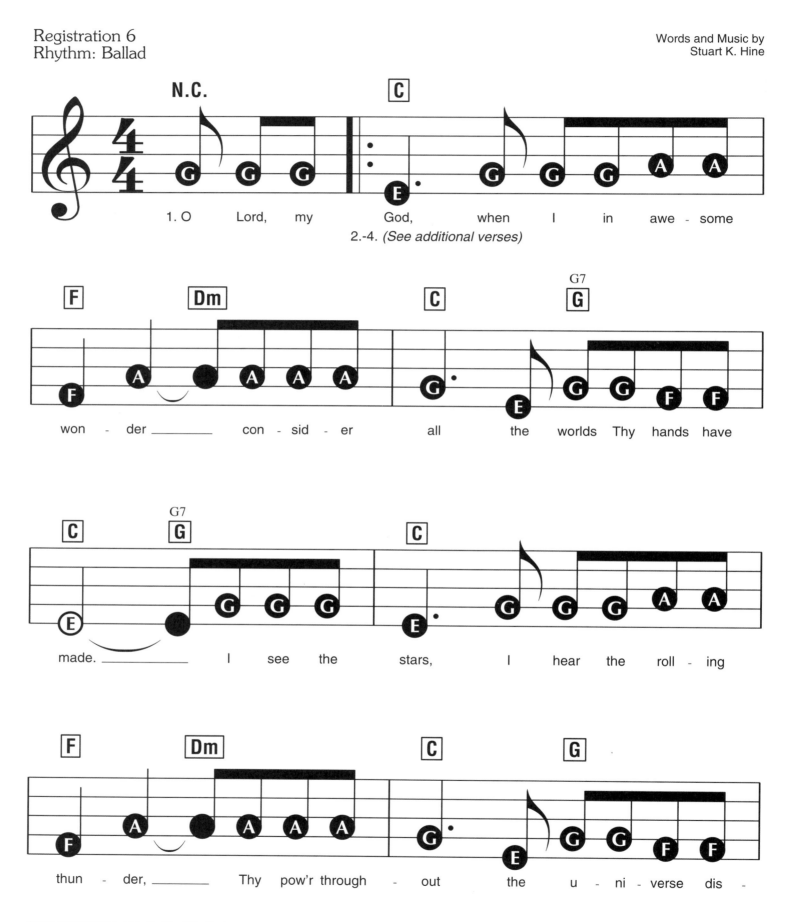

1. O Lord, my God, when I in awe - some

2.-4. *(See additional verses)*

won - der _____ con - sid - er all the worlds Thy hands have

made. _____ I see the stars, I hear the roll - ing

thun - der, _____ Thy pow'r through - out the u - ni - verse dis -

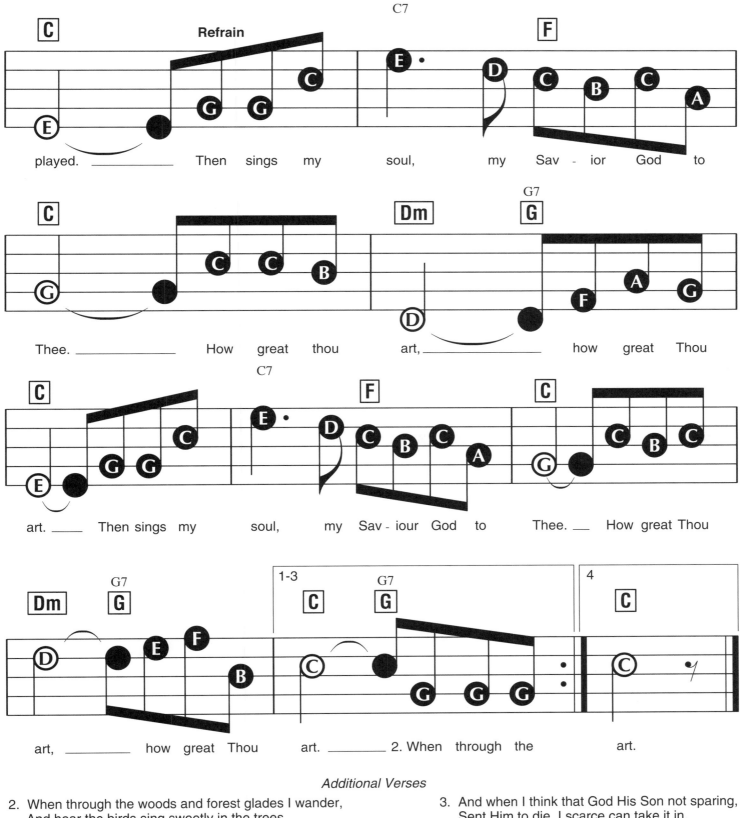

Additional Verses

2. When through the woods and forest glades I wander,
And hear the birds sing sweetly in the trees.
When I look down from lofty mountain grandeur,
And hear the brook and feel the gentle breeze.
Refrain

3. And when I think that God His Son not sparing,
Sent Him to die, I scarce can take it in.
That on the cross, my burden gladly bearing,
He bled and died to take away my sin.
Refrain

4. When Christ shall come with shout of acclamation
And take me home, what joy shall fill my heart!
Then I shall bow in humble adoration
And there proclaim my God how great Thou art.
Refrain

How Majestic Is Your Name

Registration 2
Rhythm: Rock

Words and Music by
Michael W. Smith

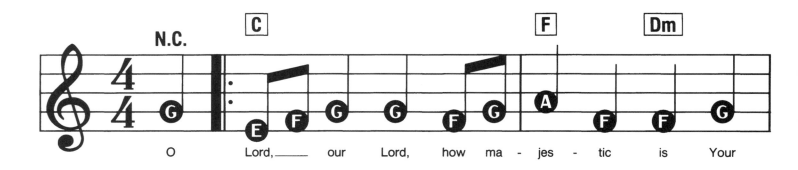

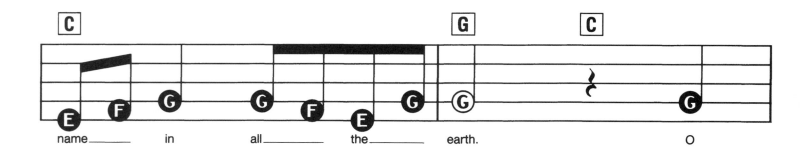

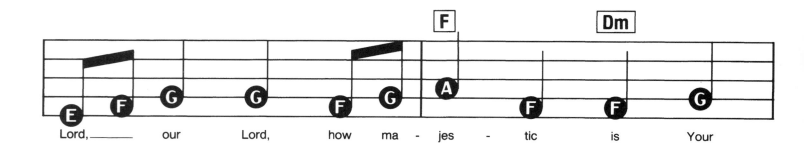

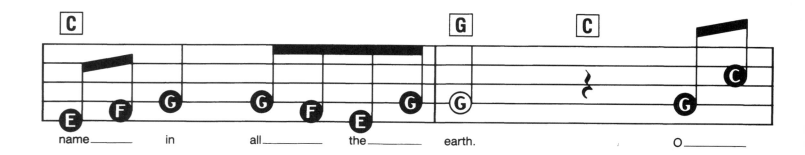

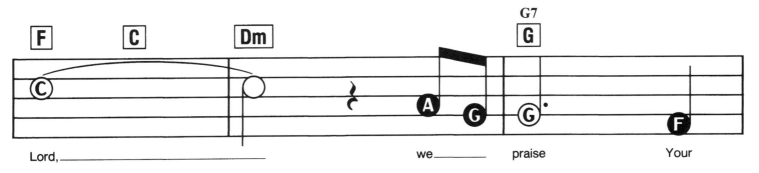

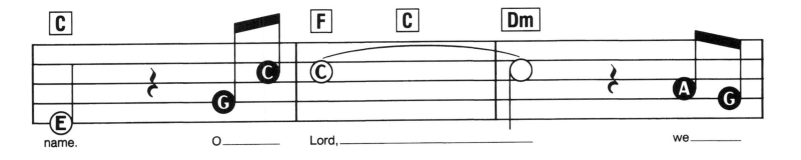

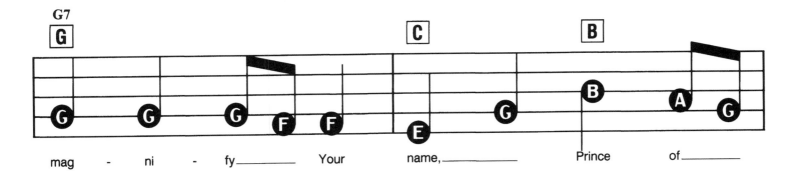

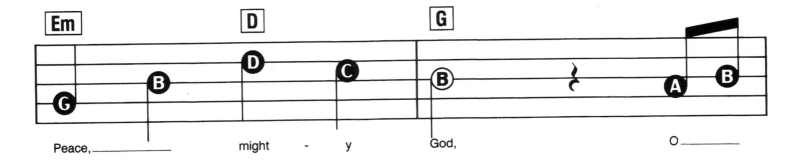

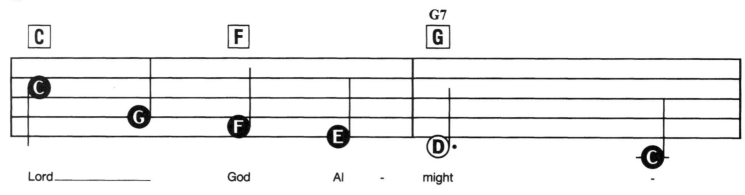

Lord_____ God Al - might

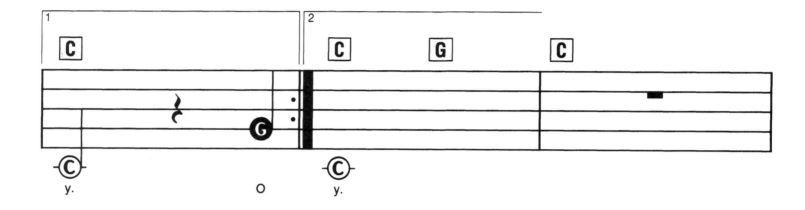

y. O y.

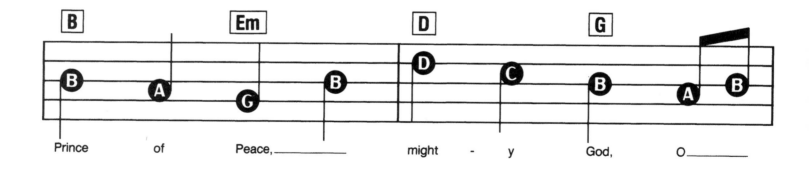

Prince of Peace,_____ might - y God, O_____

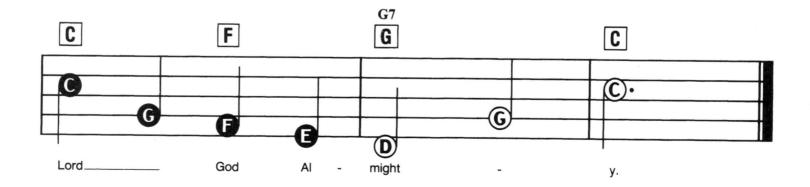

Lord_____ God Al - might - y.

How Great Is Our God

Registration 4
Rhythm: 8-Beat or Ballad

Words and Music by Chris Tomlin,
Jesse Reeves and Ed Cash

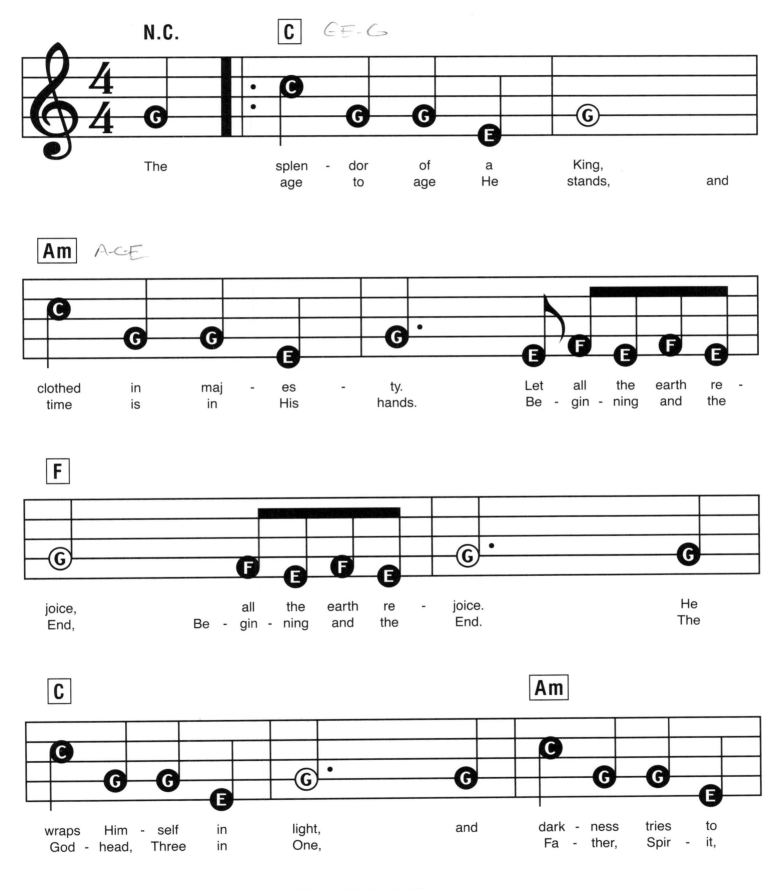

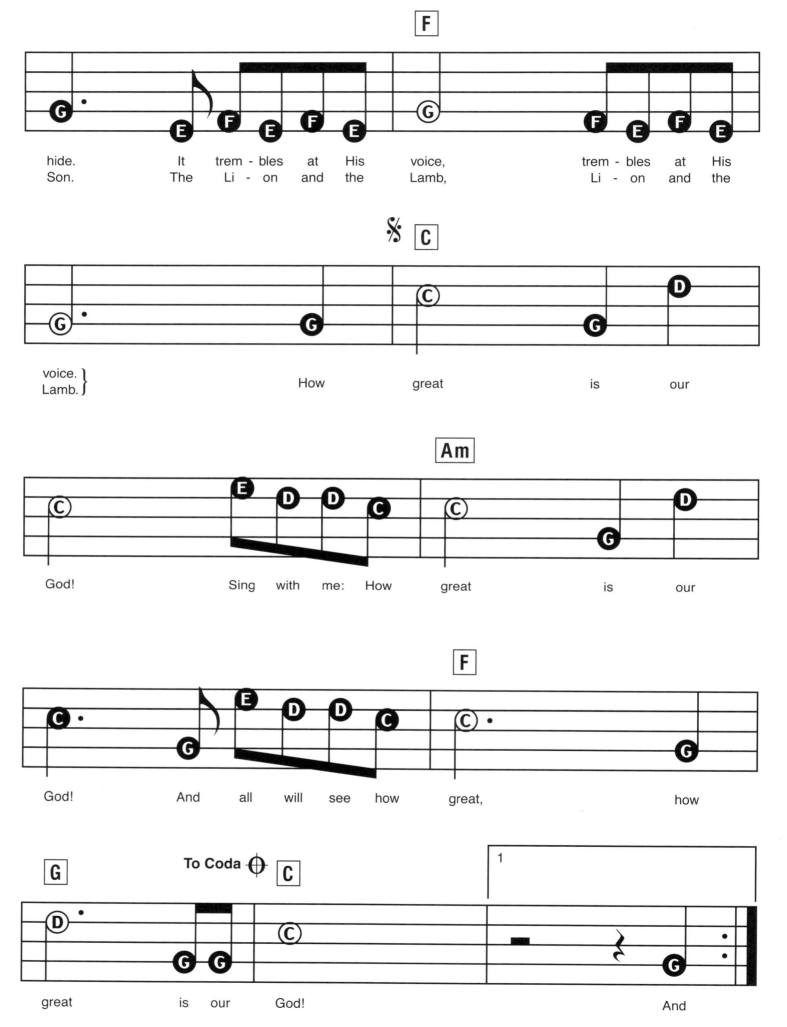

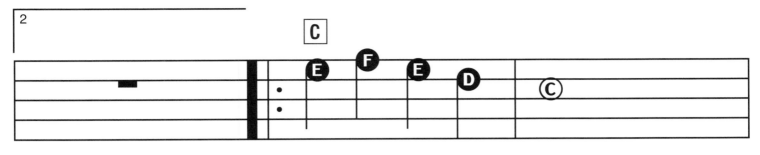

Name a - bove all   names,

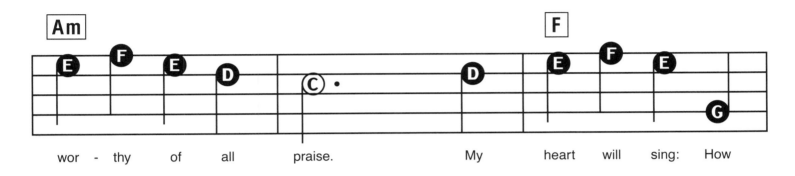

wor - thy of all   praise.   My   heart will   sing: How

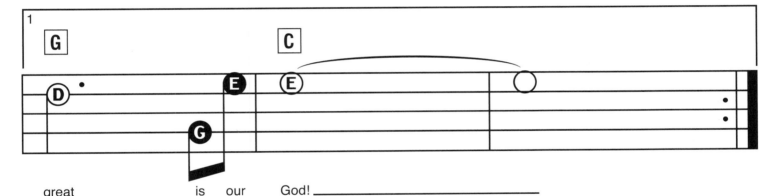

great   is   our   God! _____

D.S. al Coda
(Return to ℅
Play to ⊕ and
Skip to Coda)

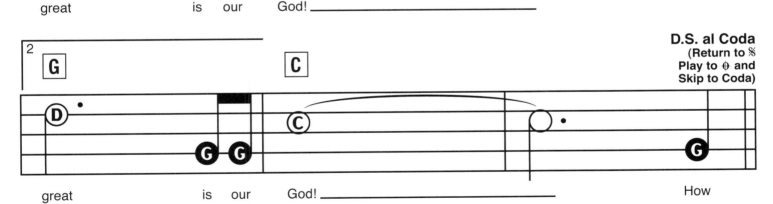

great   is   our   God! _____   How

CODA
⊕ C

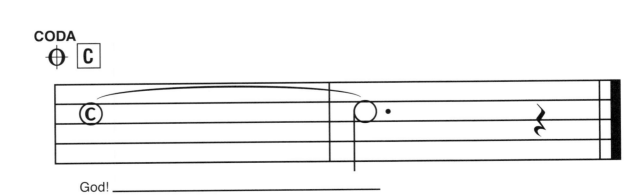

God! _____

I Come to the Cross

Registration 1
Rhythm: Waltz

Words and Music by Bill Batstone
and Bob Somma

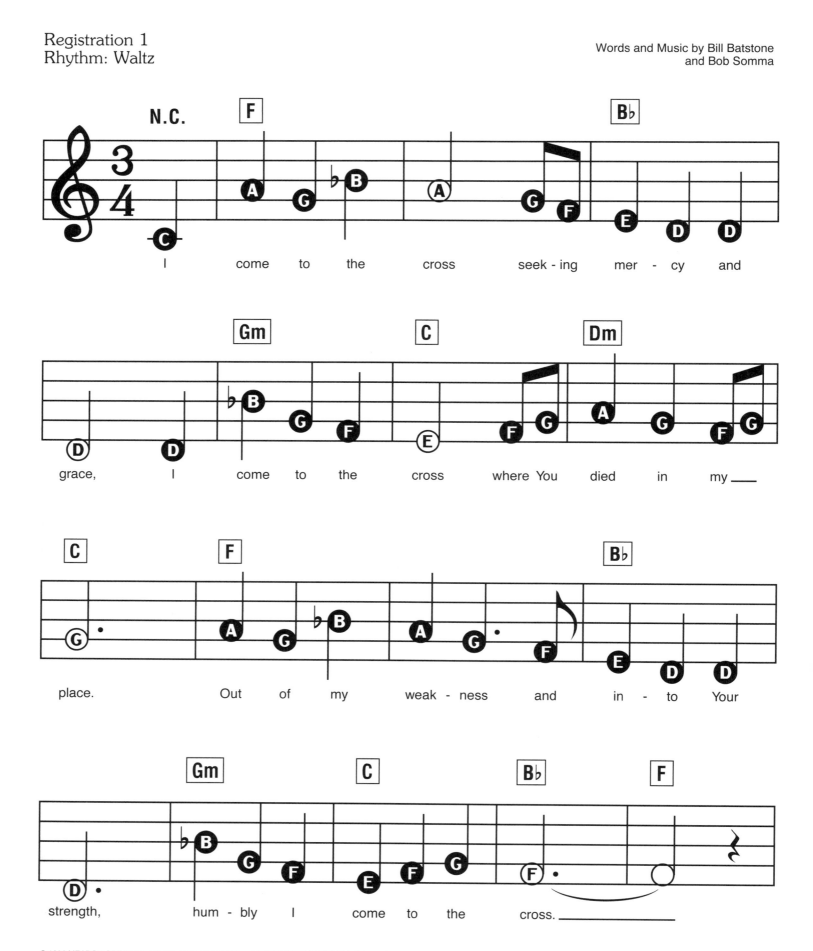

I Need You More

Registration 1
Rhythm: Ballad or Pop

Words and Music by Lindell Cooley
and Bruce Haynes

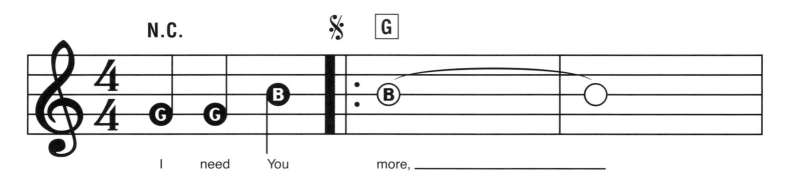

N.C.   𝄋   G

I need You   more, _____

Am

more   than   yes - ter - day.   I   need   You

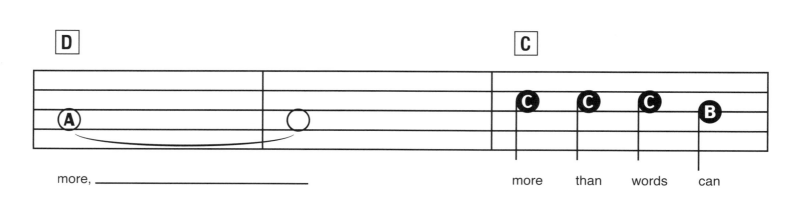

D   C

more, _____   more   than   words   can

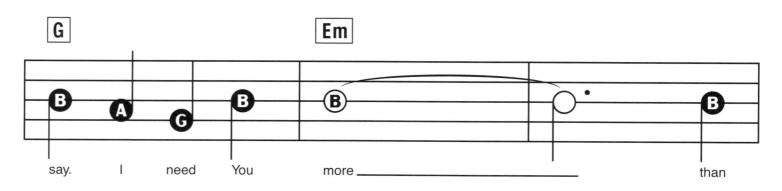

G   Em

say.   I   need   You   more _____   than

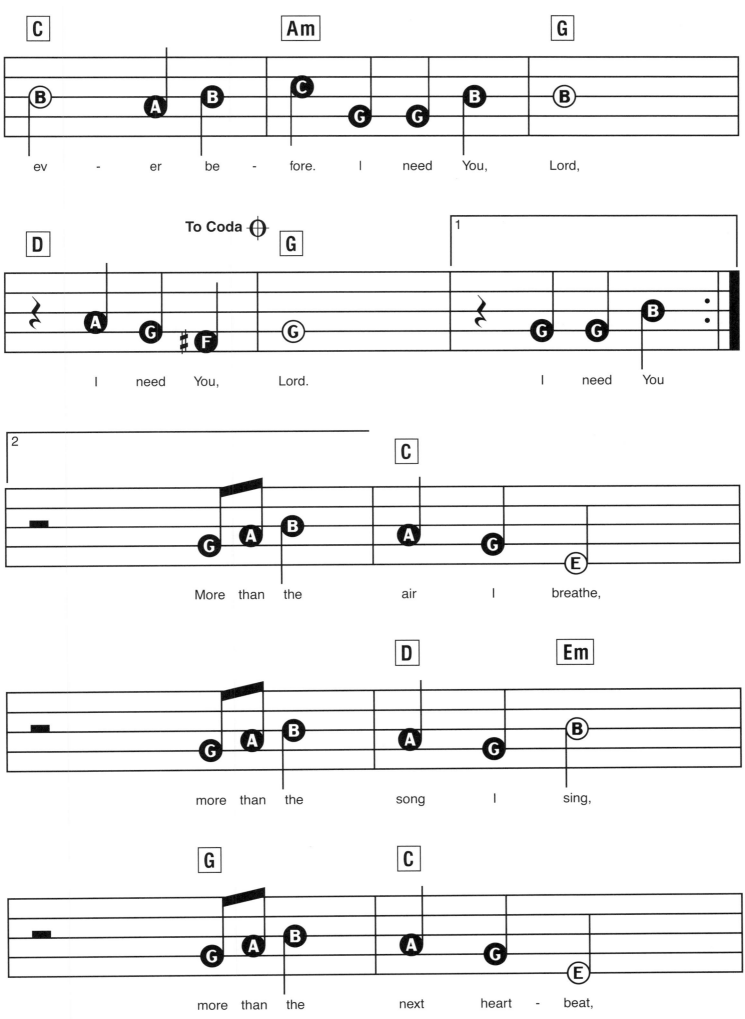

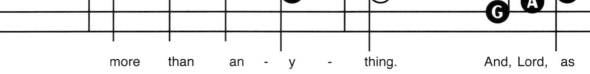

G

more than an - y - thing. And, Lord, as

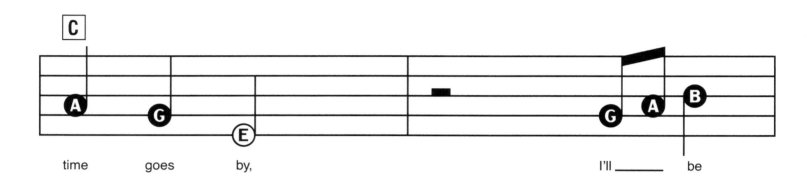

C

time goes by, I'll _____ be

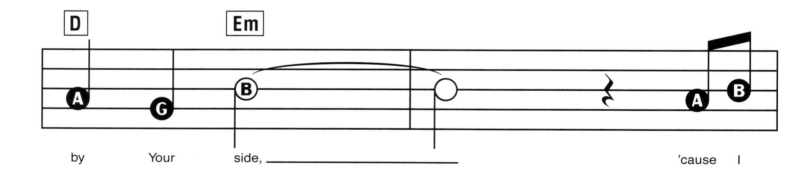

D   **Em**

by Your side, _____ 'cause I

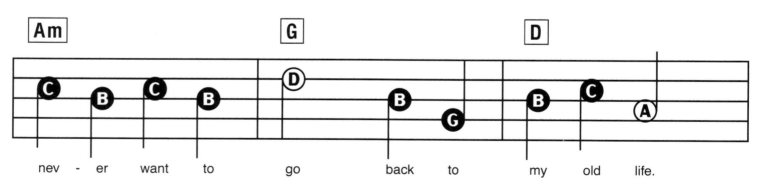

Am   **G**   **D**

nev - er want to go back to my old life.

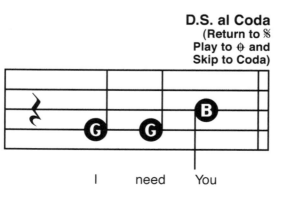

D.S. al Coda
(Return to %
Play to ⊕ and
Skip to Coda)

I need You

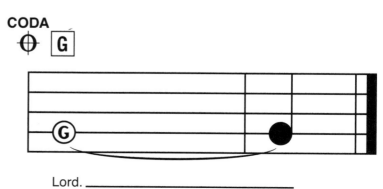

CODA
⊕ **G**

Lord. _____

Jesus, Lord to Me

Registration 3
Rhythm: Ballad

Words and Music by Greg Nelson
and Gary McSpadden

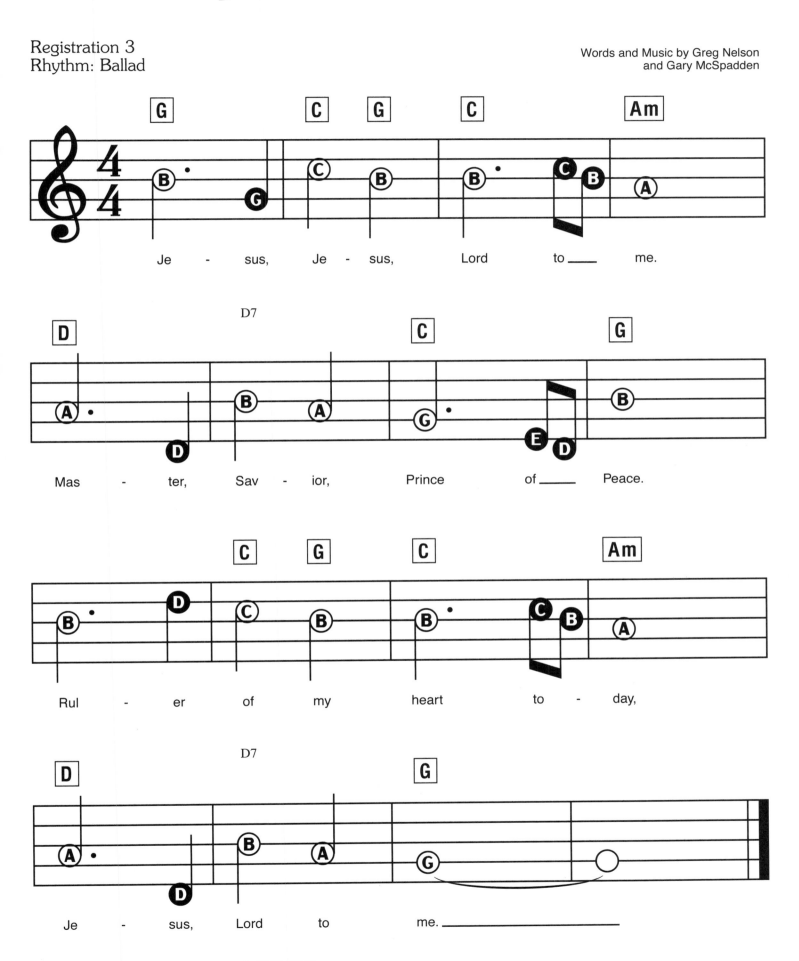

I Sing Praises

Registration 3
Rhythm: Ballad or 8-Beat

Words and Music by
Terry MacAlmon

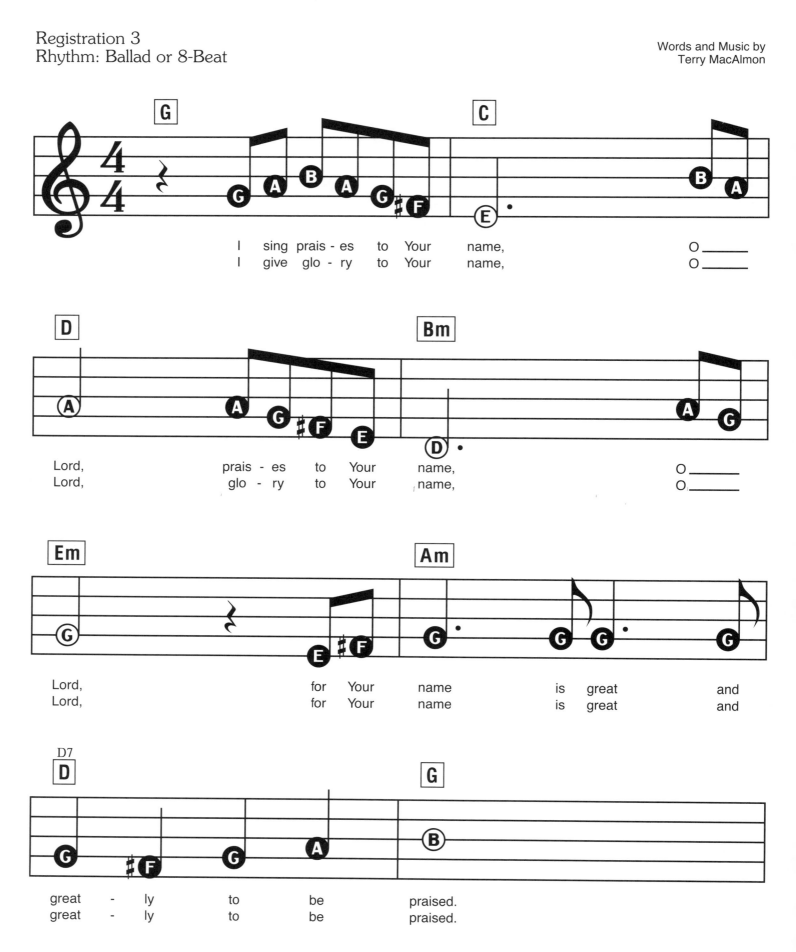

I Will Call Upon the Lord

Registration 2
Rhythm: Rock or 8-Beat

Words and Music by
Michael O'Shields

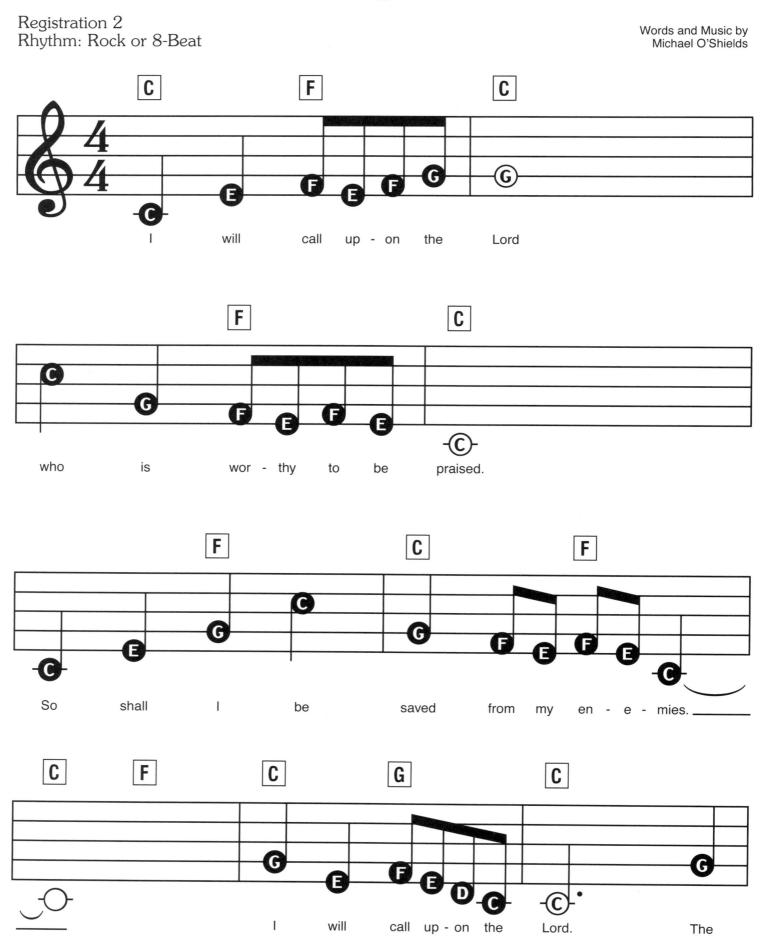

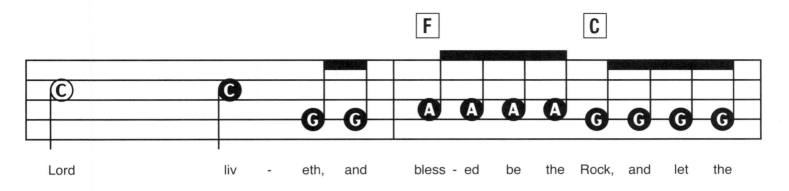

Lord   liv - eth, and   bless - ed   be   the   Rock,   and   let   the

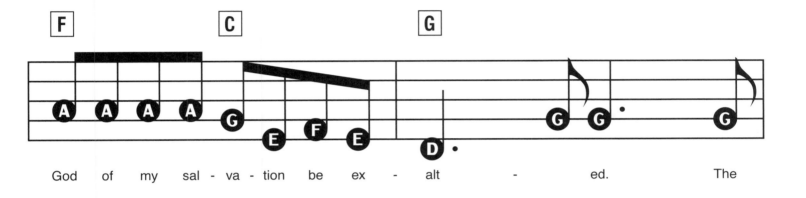

God   of   my   sal - va - tion   be   ex - alt   -   ed.   The

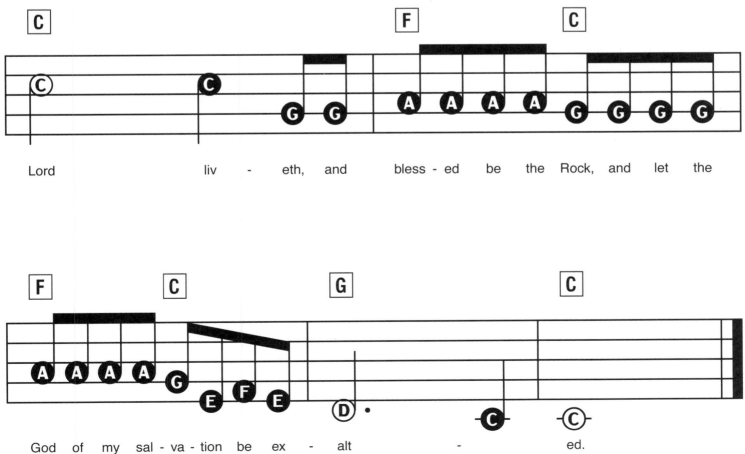

Lord   liv - eth, and   bless - ed   be   the   Rock,   and   let   the

God   of   my   sal - va - tion   be   ex - alt   -   ed.

I Will Celebrate

Registration 7
Rhythm: Pop or 16-Beat

Words and Music by
Rita Baloche

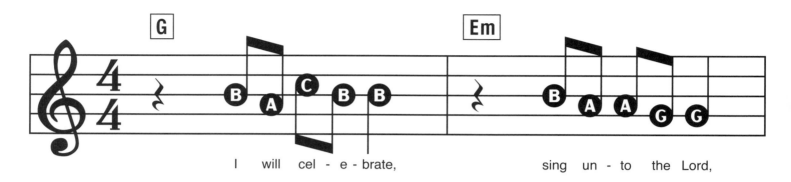

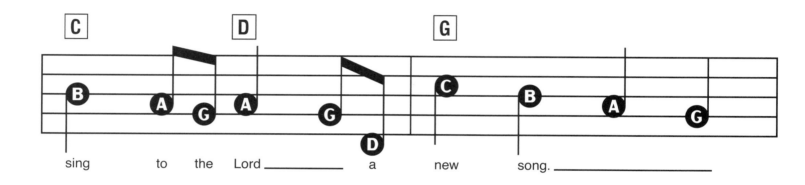

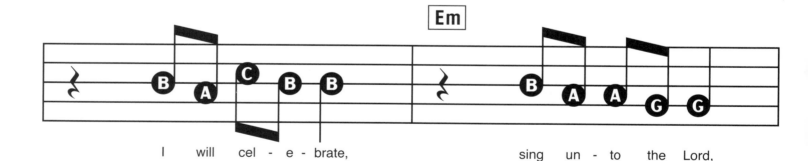

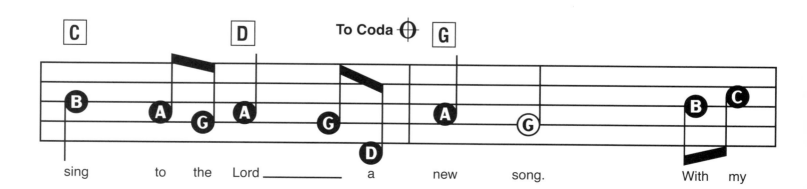

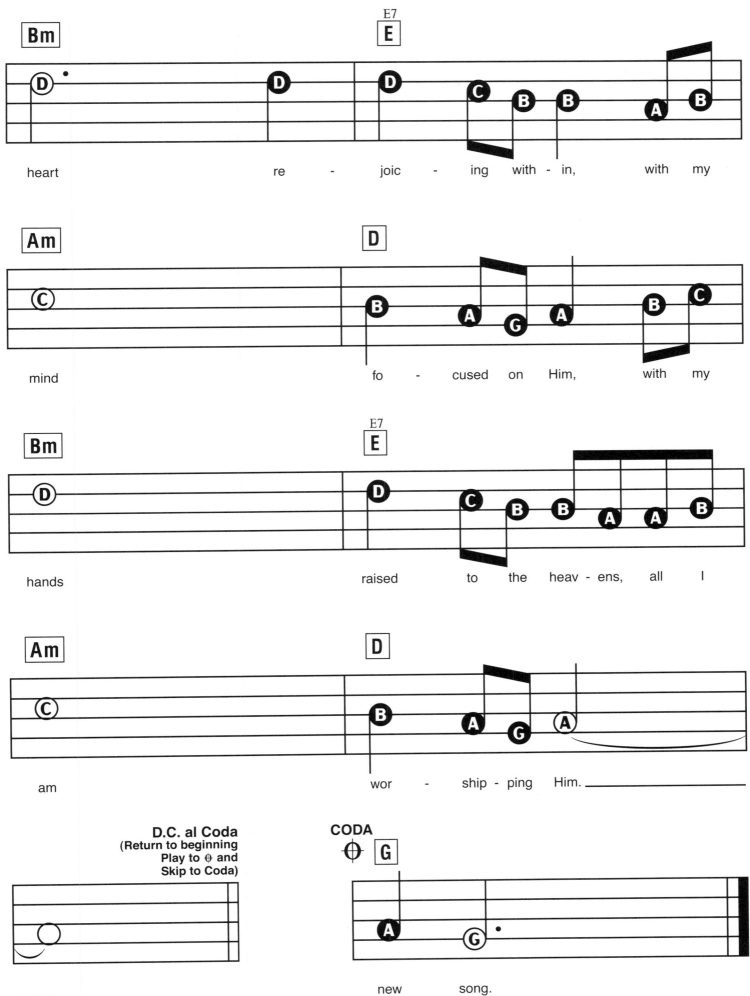

In Christ Alone

Registration 1
Rhythm: None

Words and Music by Keith Getty
and Stuart Townend

In Christ a - lone my hope is found, He is my
lone, who took on flesh, full - ness of
ground His bod - y lay, Light of the
life, no fear in death; this is the

light, my strength, my song. This cor - ner -
God in help - less babe! This gift of
world by dark - ness slain. Then burst - ing
pow'r of Christ in me. From life's first

stone, this sol - id ground, firm through the
love and right - eous - ness, scorned by the
forth and in glo - rious day, up from the
cry to fi - nal breath, Je - sus com -

fierc - est drought and storm. What heights of
ones He came to save. Till on of
grave He rose a - gain! And as He
mands my des - ti - ny. No pow'r of

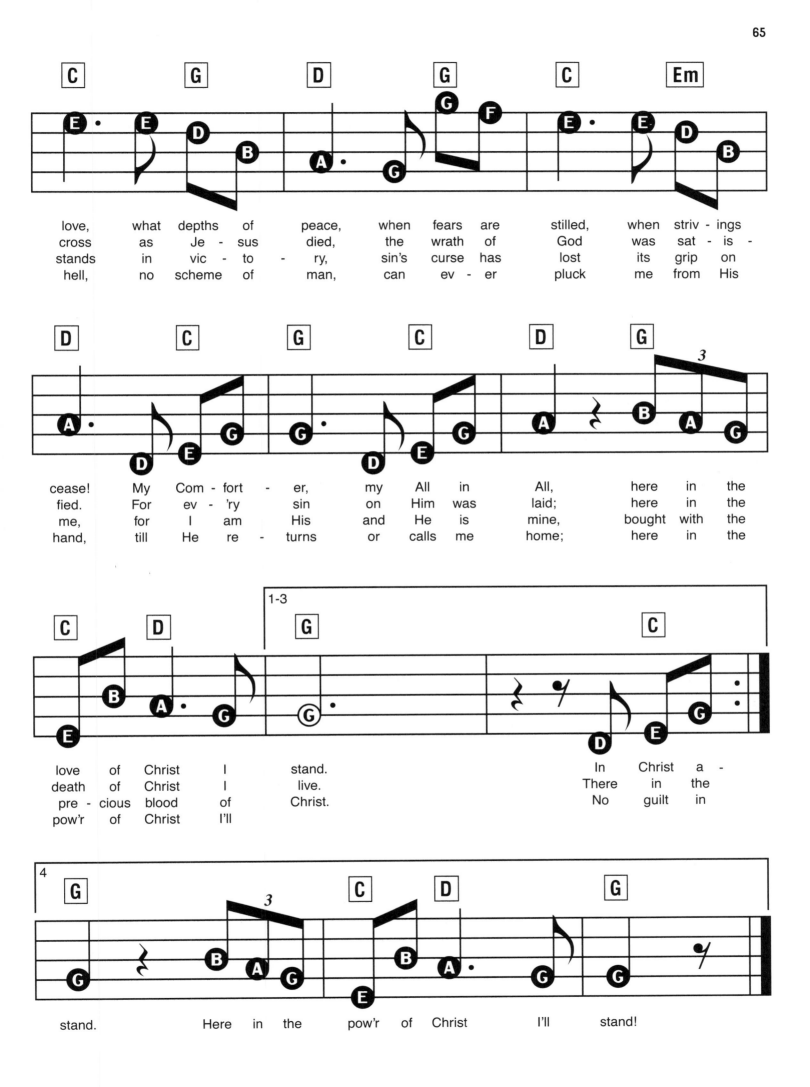

Lord, I Lift Your Name on High

Registration 7
Rhythm: Pop or 16-Beat

Words and Music by
Rick Founds

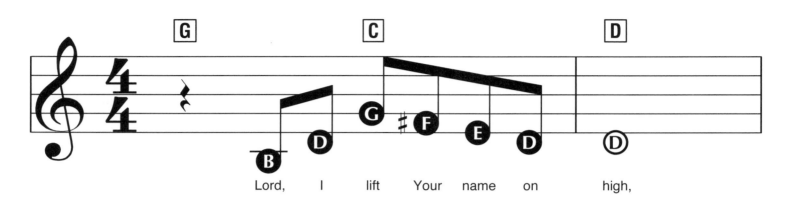

Lord, I lift Your name on high,

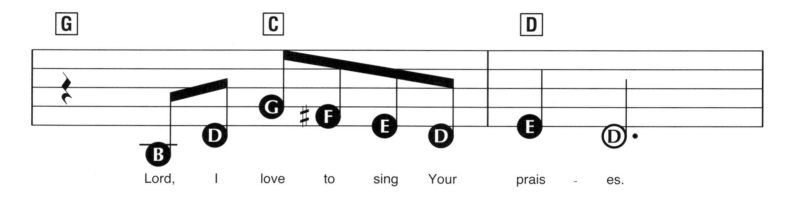

Lord, I love to sing Your prais - es.

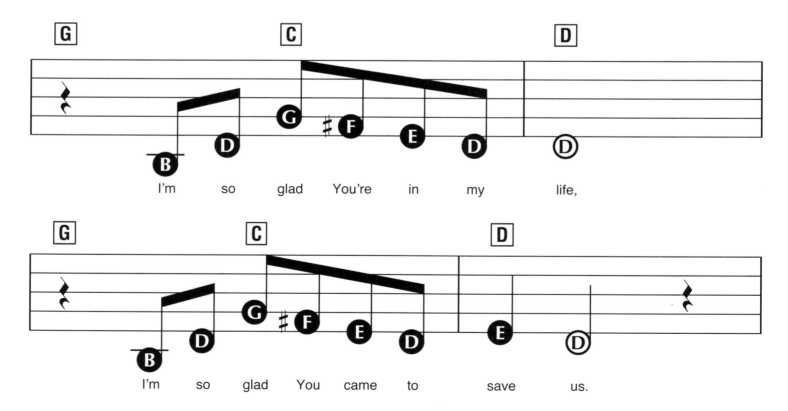

I'm so glad You're in my life,

I'm so glad You came to save us.

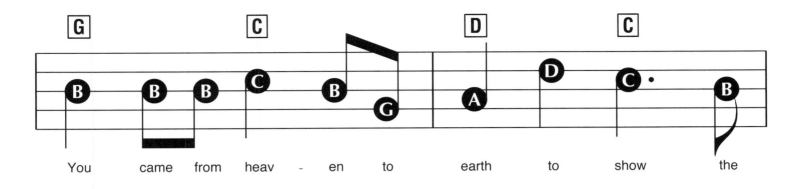

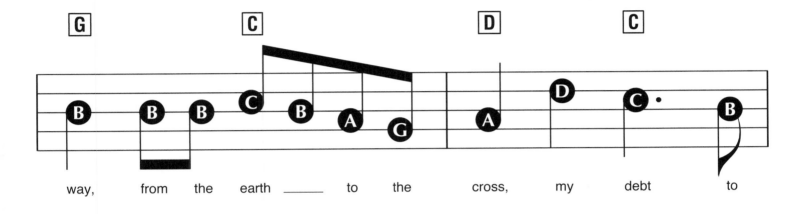

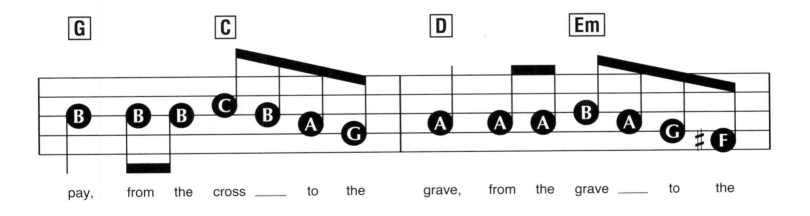

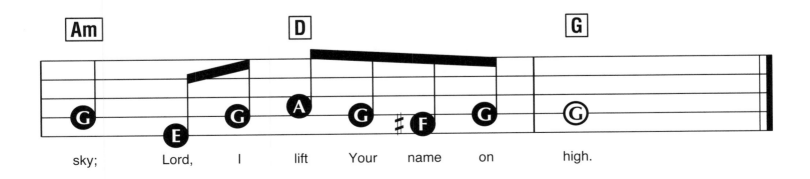

The Lord Reigns

Registration 7
Rhythm: 8-Beat or Rock

Words and Music by
Dan Stradwick

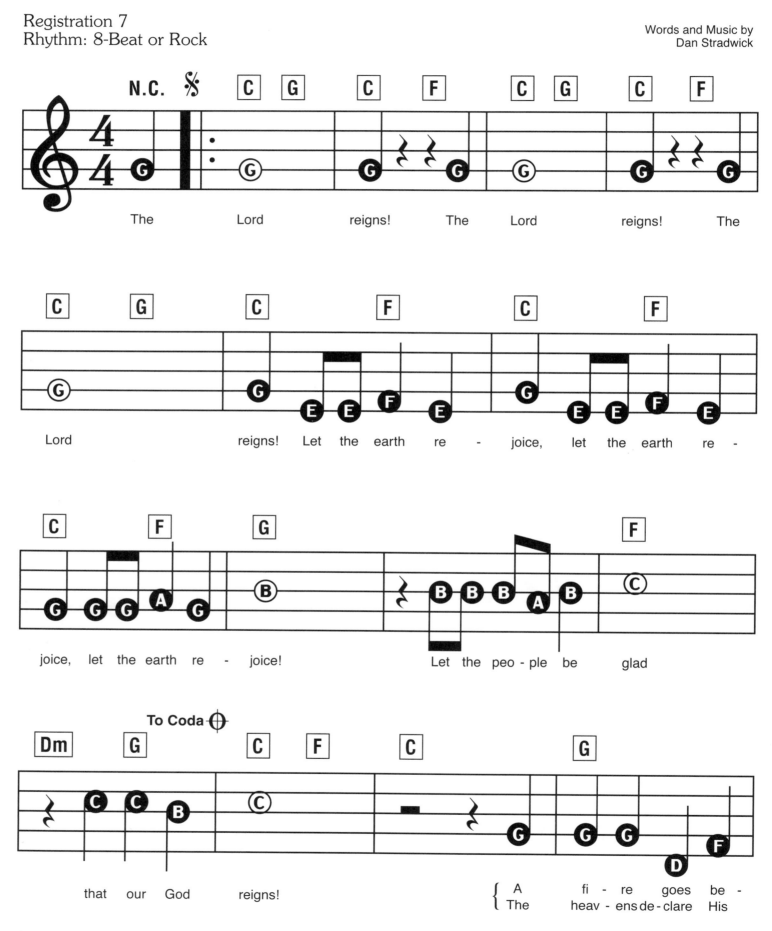

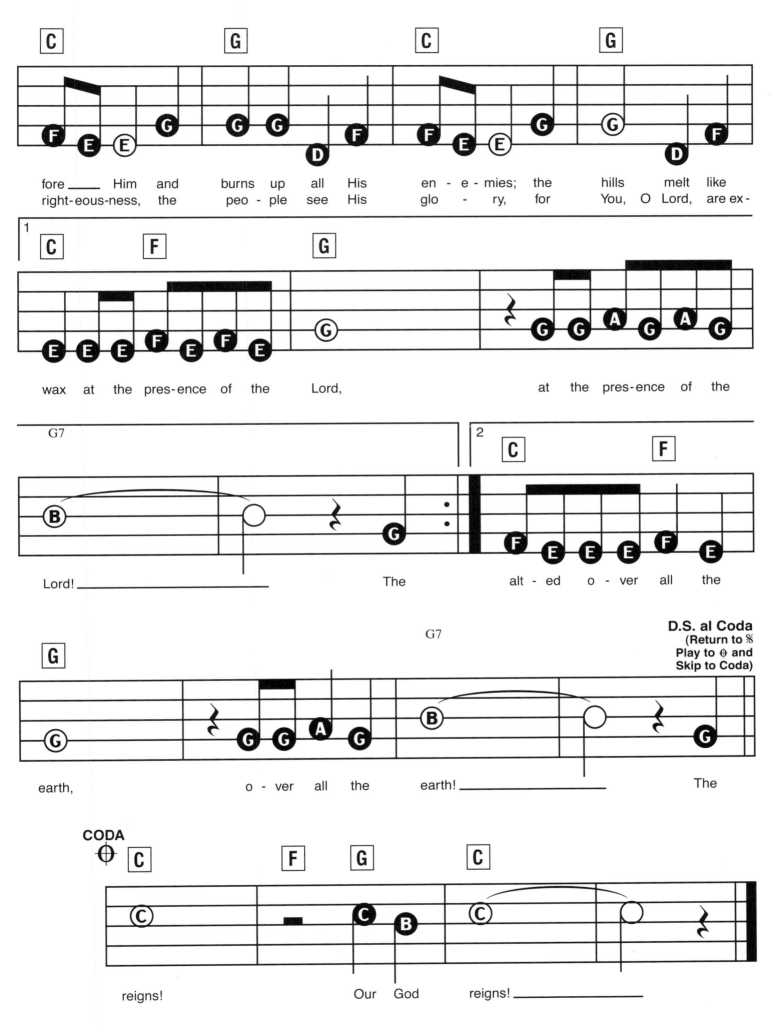

More Precious Than Silver

Registration 1
Rhythm: Ballad

Words and Music by
Lynn DeShazo

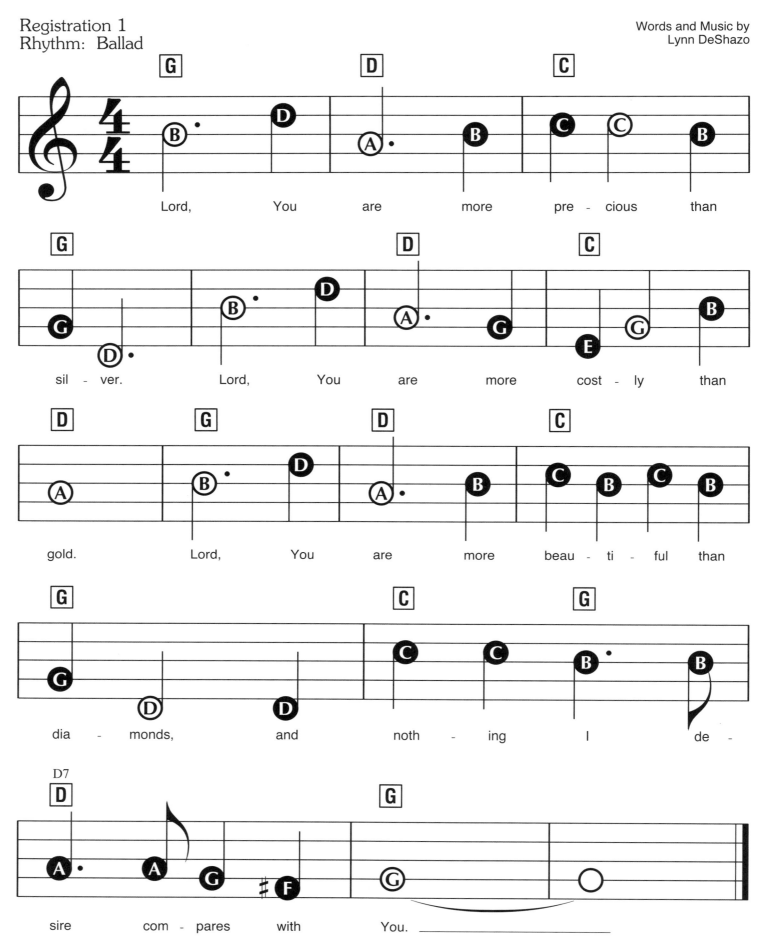

Open the Eyes of My Heart

Registration 8
Rhythm: 8-Beat or Rock

Words and Music by
Paul Baloche

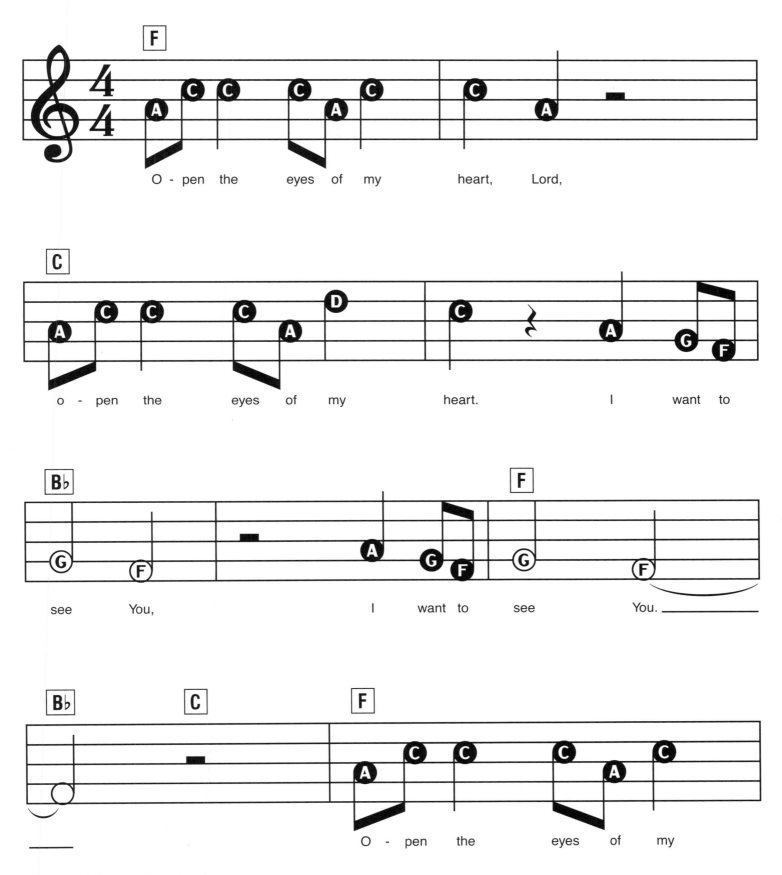

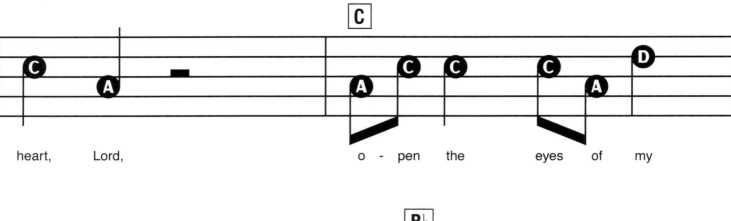

heart, Lord, o - pen the eyes of my

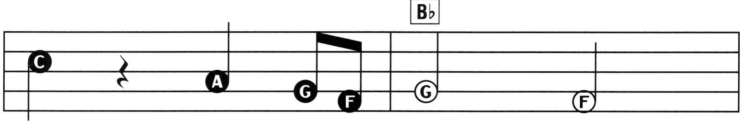

heart. I want to see You,

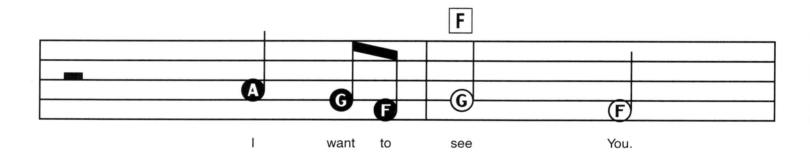

I want to see You.

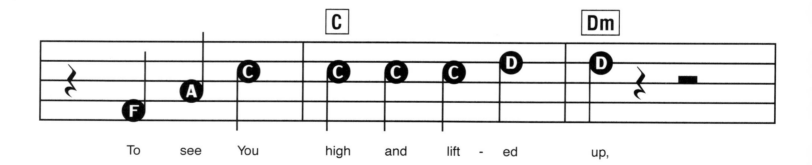

To see You high and lift - ed up,

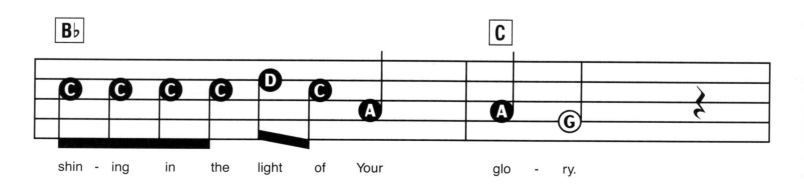

shin - ing in the light of Your glo - ry.

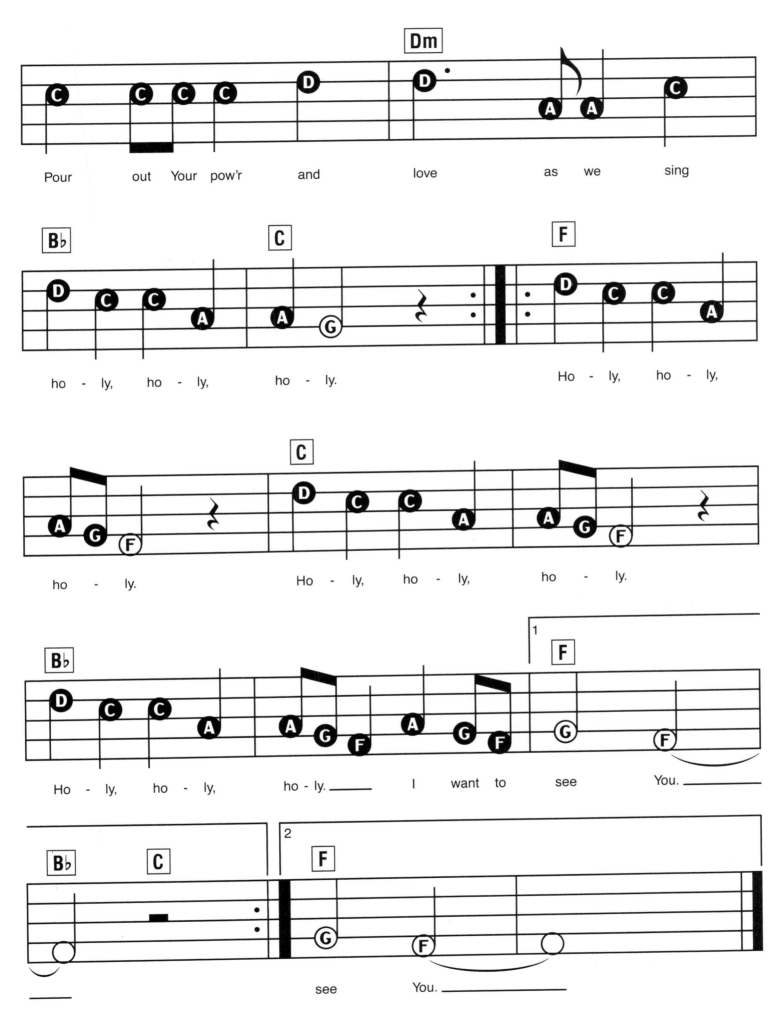

O Magnify the Lord

Registration 2
Rhythm: March or Pop

Words and Music by Melodie Tunney
and Dick Tunney

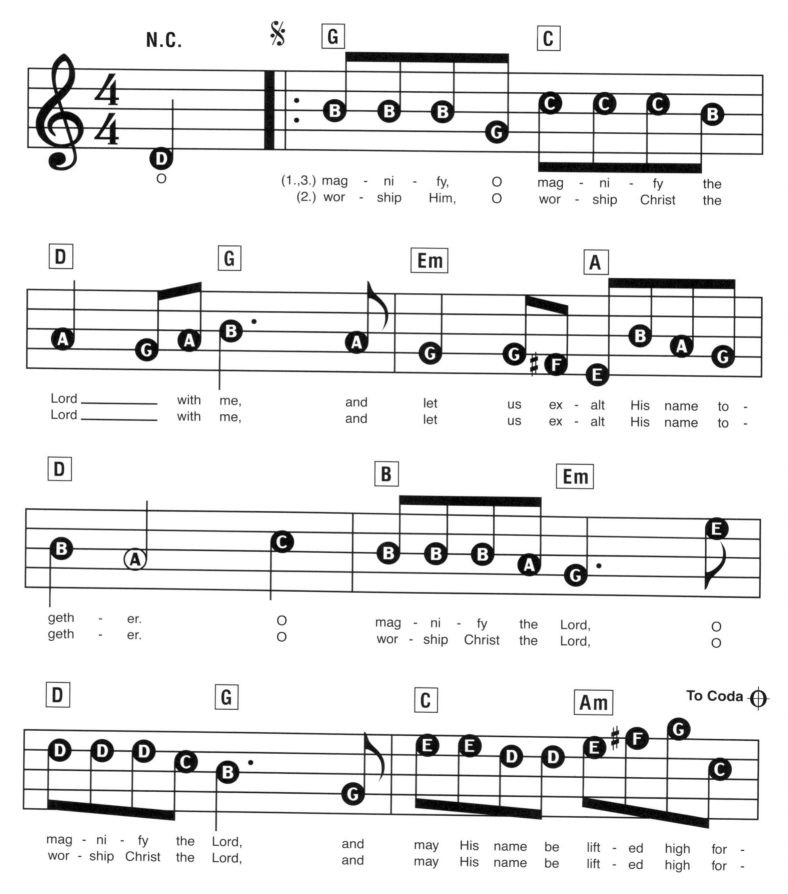

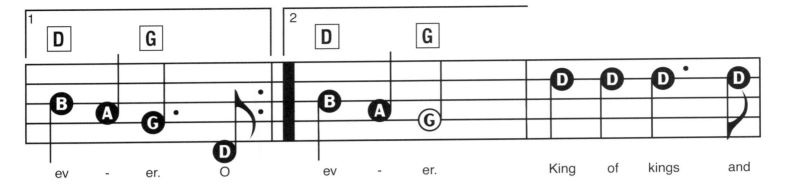

ev - er. O   ev - er.   King of kings and

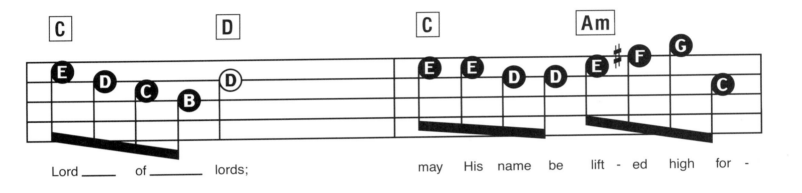

Lord _____ of _____ lords;   may His name be lift - ed high for -

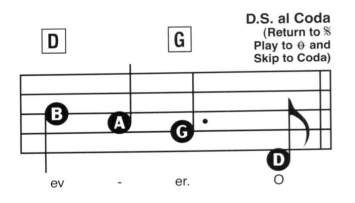

D.S. al Coda
(Return to 𝄋
Play to ⊕ and
Skip to Coda)

ev - er.   O

CODA

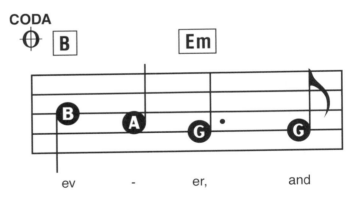

ev - er,   and

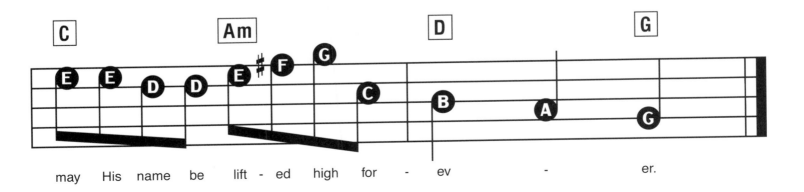

may His name be lift - ed high for - ev - er.

Oh Lord, You're Beautiful

Registration 3
Rhythm: Ballad

Words and Music by
Keith Green

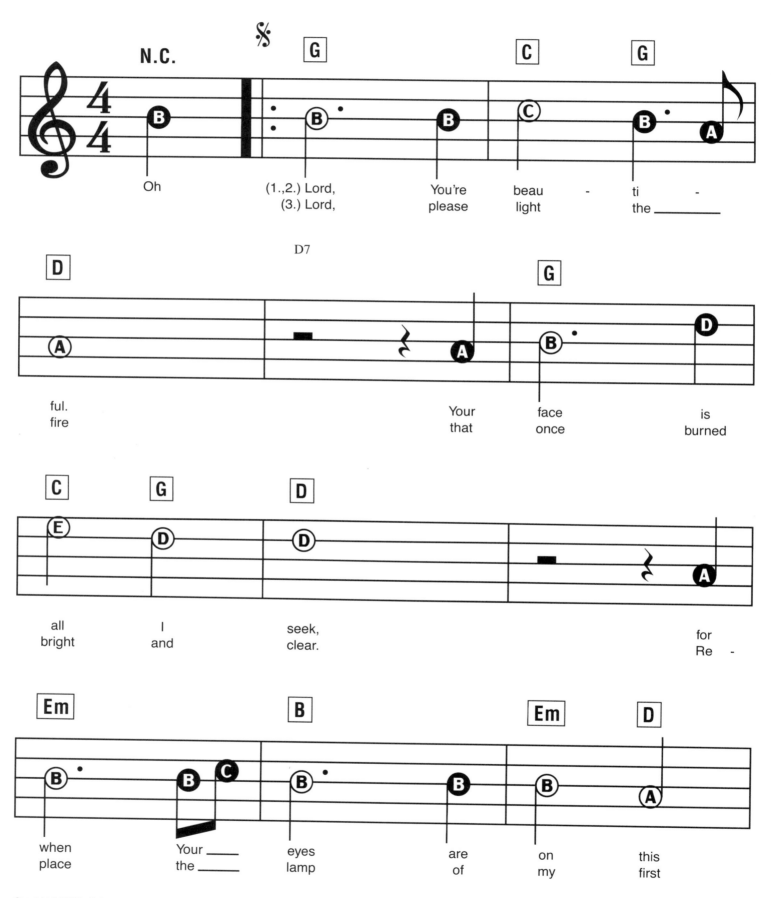

77

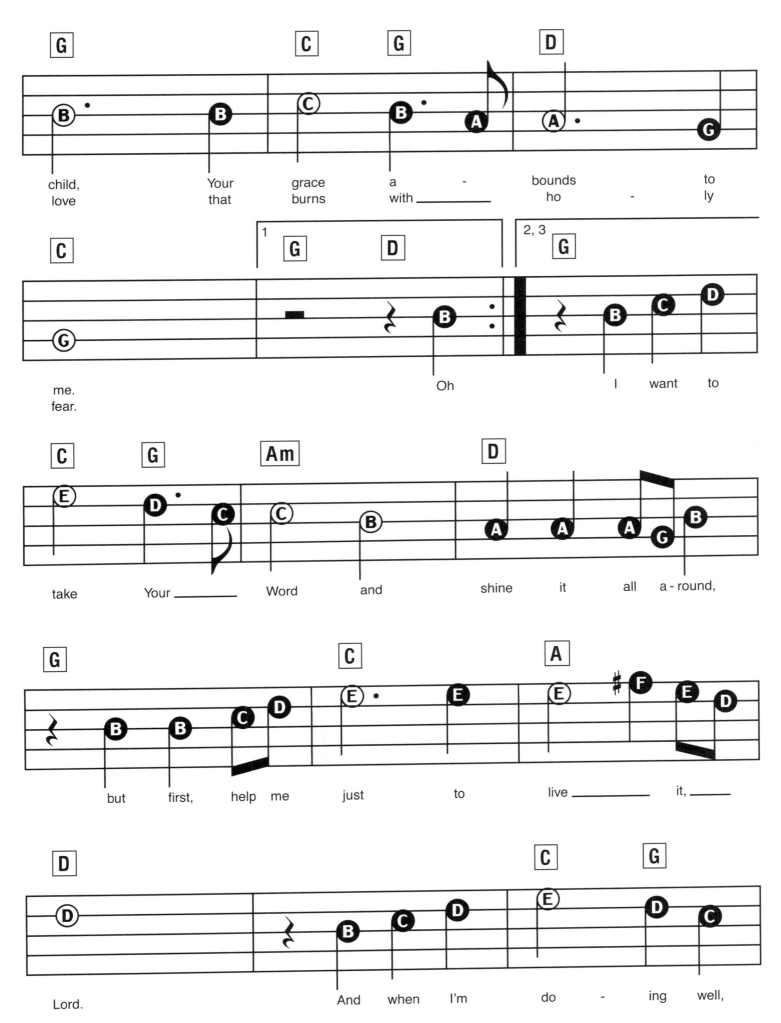

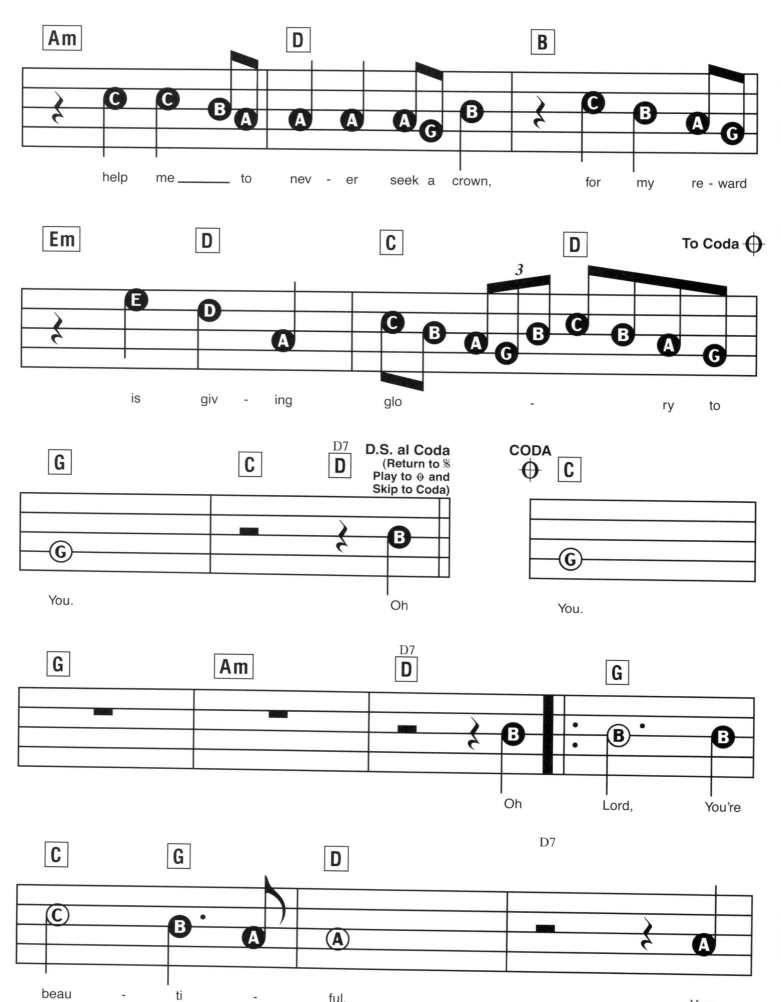

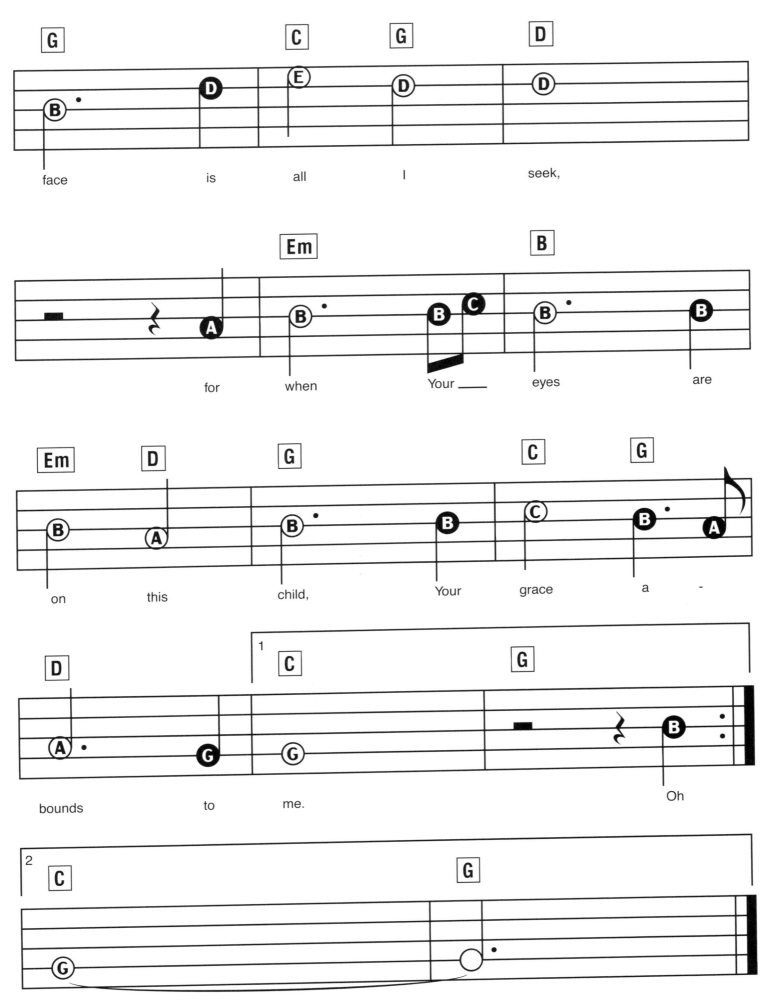

Open Our Eyes

Registration 3
Rhythm: Waltz

Words and Music by
Bob Cull

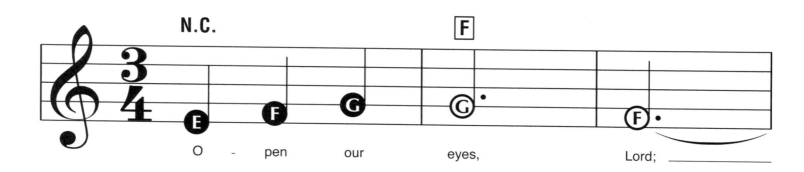

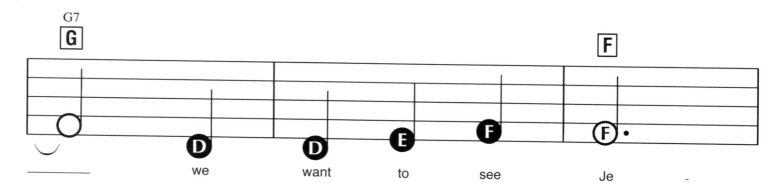

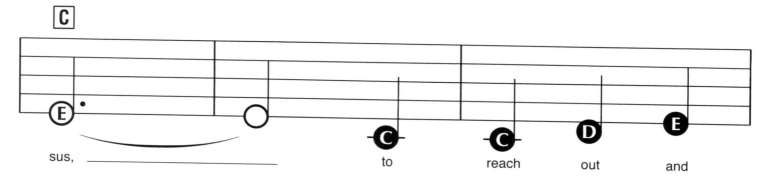

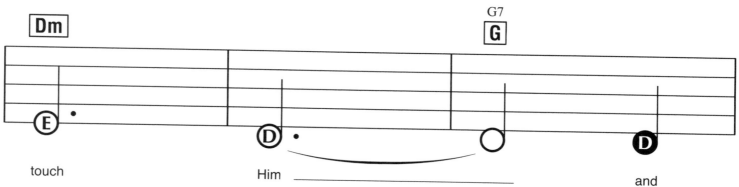

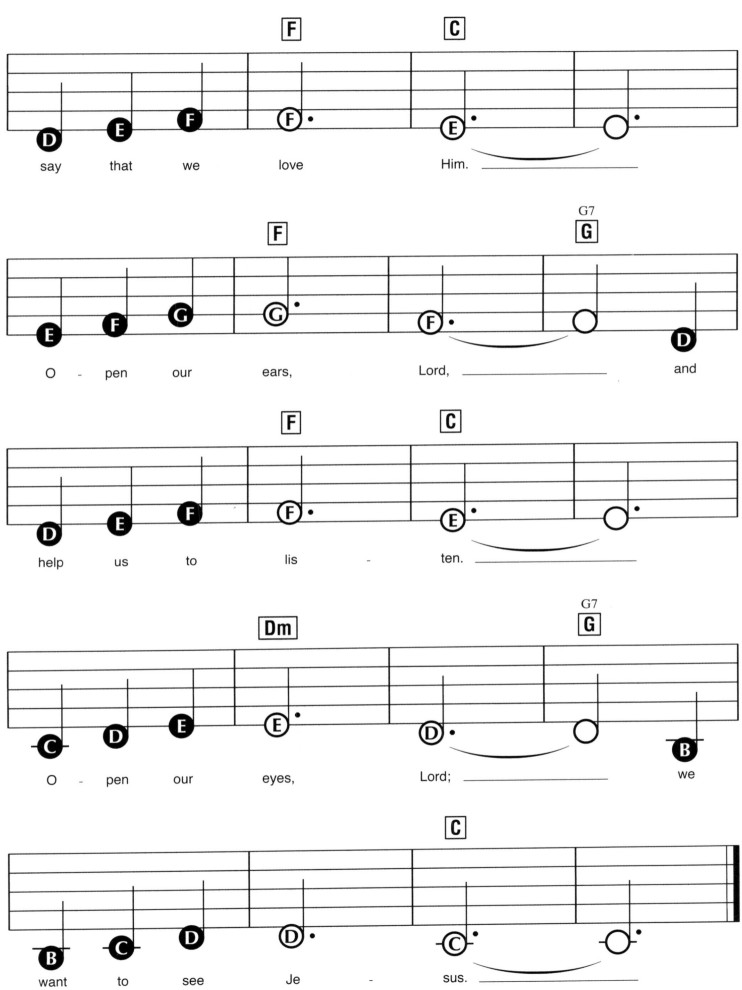

Rise Up and Praise Him

Registration 7
Rhythm: Pop or 8-Beat

Words and Music by Paul Baloche
and Gary Sadler

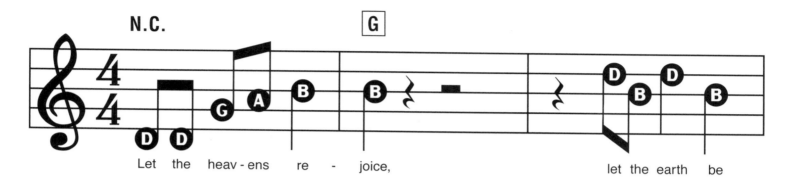

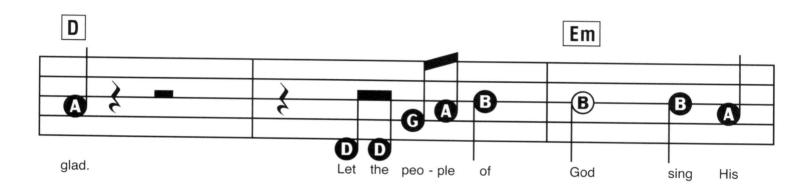

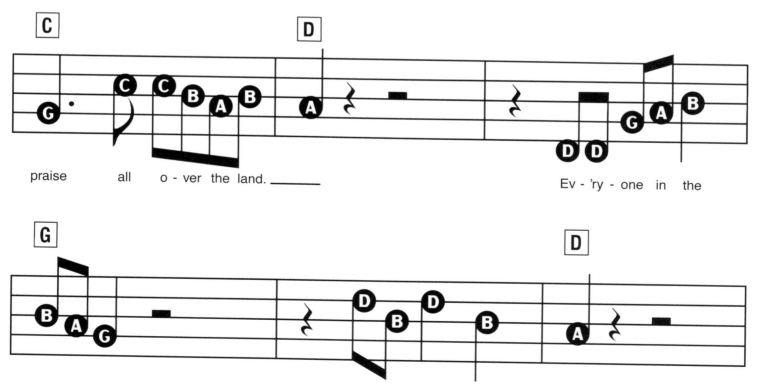

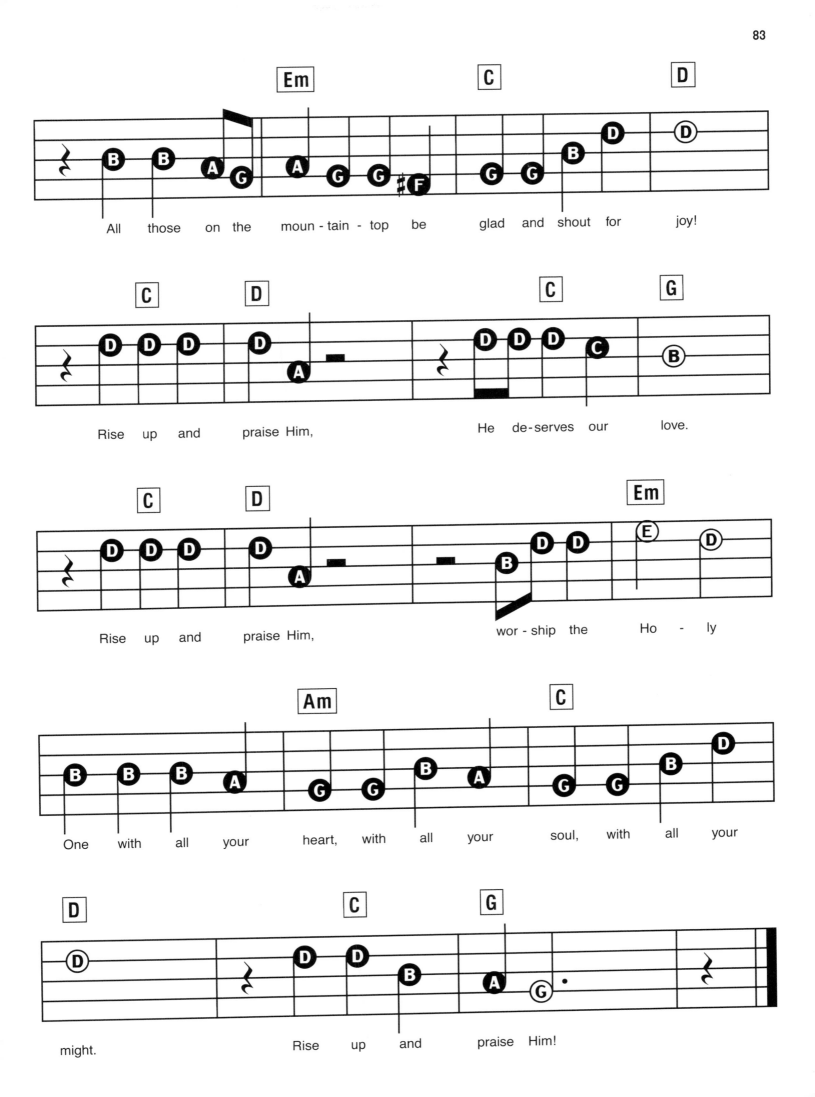

Shine, Jesus, Shine

Registration 2
Rhythm: 16-Beat or Disco

Words and Music by
Graham Kendrick

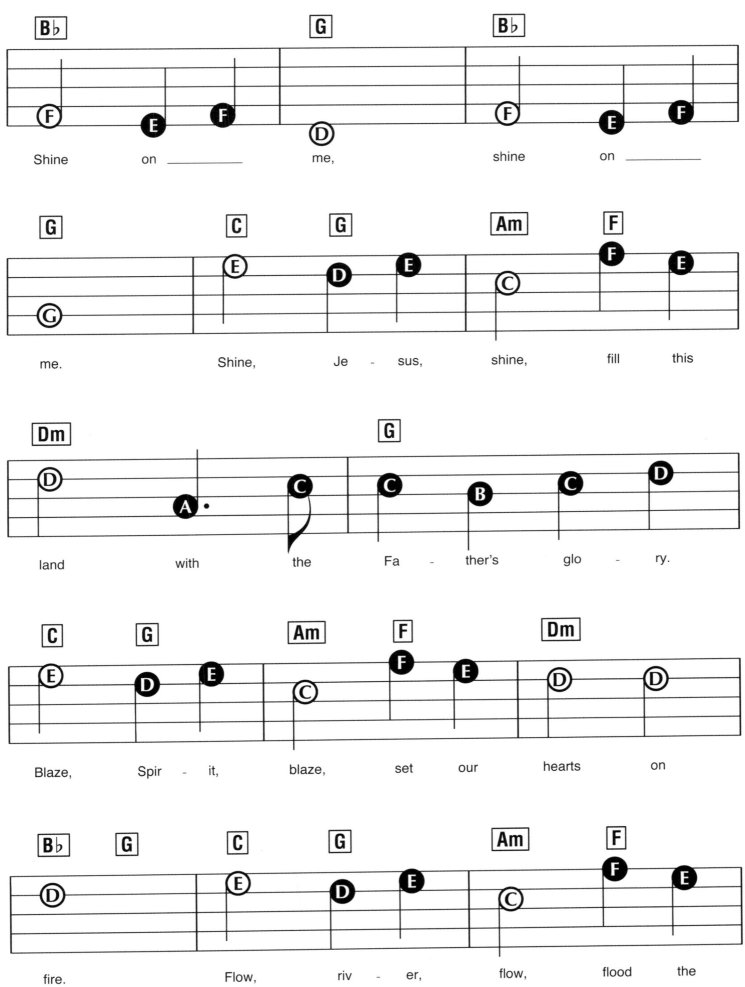

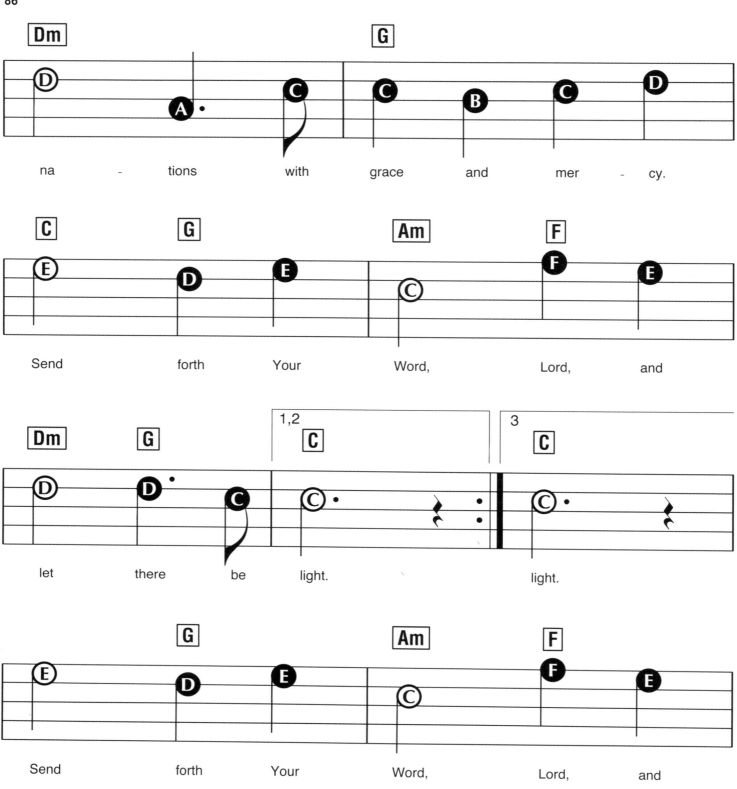

na - tions   with   grace   and   mer - cy.

Send   forth   Your   Word,   Lord,   and

1,2   **C**   **3**   **C**

let   there   be   light.   light.

Send   forth   Your   Word,   Lord,   and

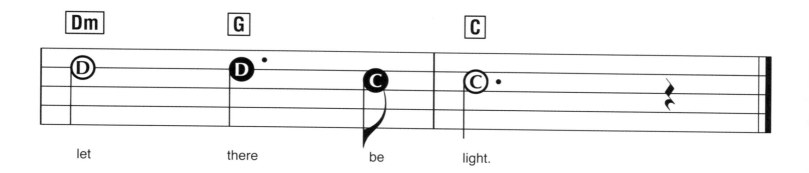

let   there   be   light.

The Potter's Hand

Registration 1
Rhythm: Ballad or 8-Beat

Words and Music by
Darlene Zschech

Beau - ti - ful   Lord,   won - der - ful   Sav - ior,

I know for   sure,   all of my   days   are   held in Your   hand,

craft - ed   in - to   Your   per - fect   plan. _____

You gen - tly   call   me   in - to Your   pres - ence,   guid - ing me   by

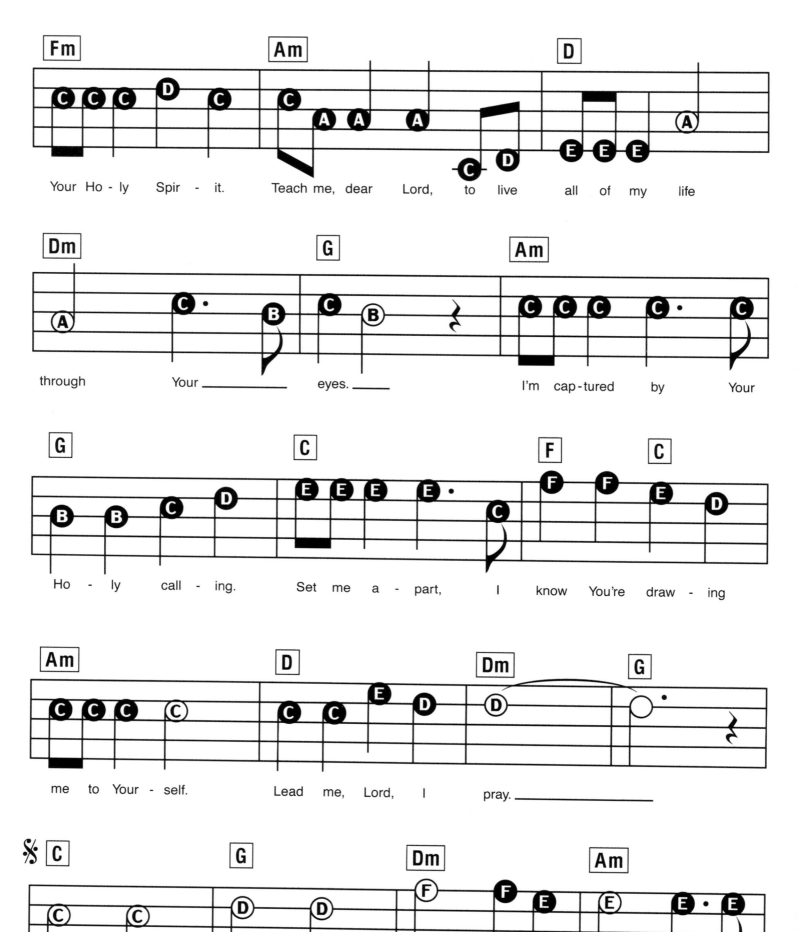

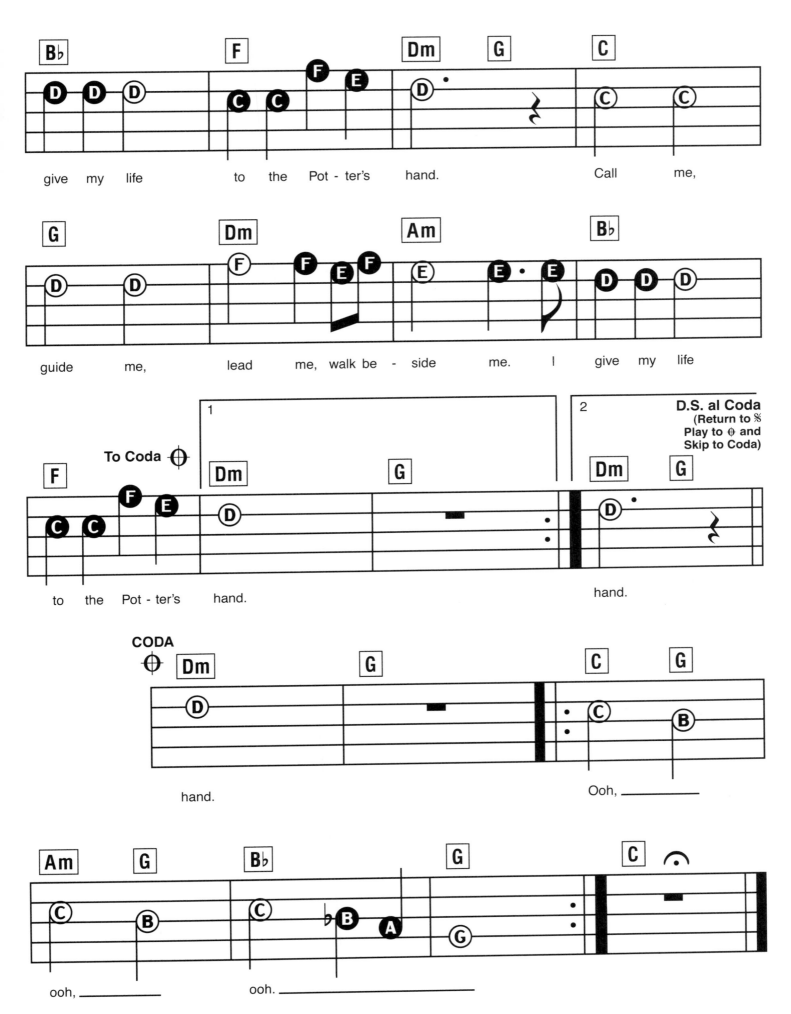

Spirit of the Living God

Registration 1
Rhythm: Ballad or 8-Beat

Words and Music by Daniel Iverson
and Lowell Alexander

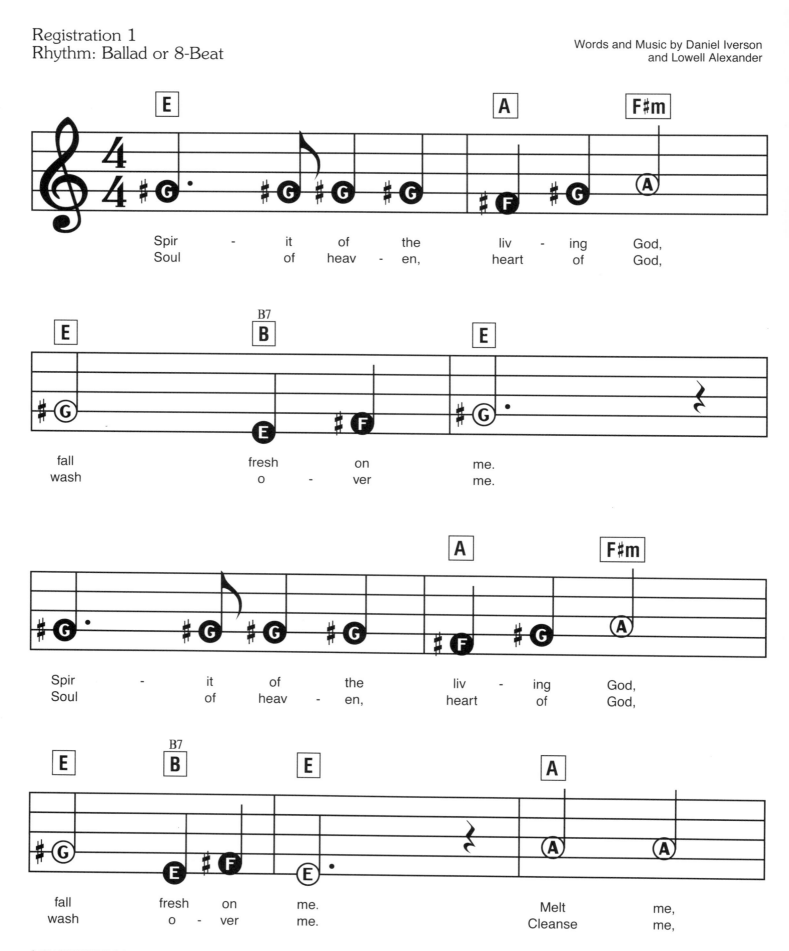

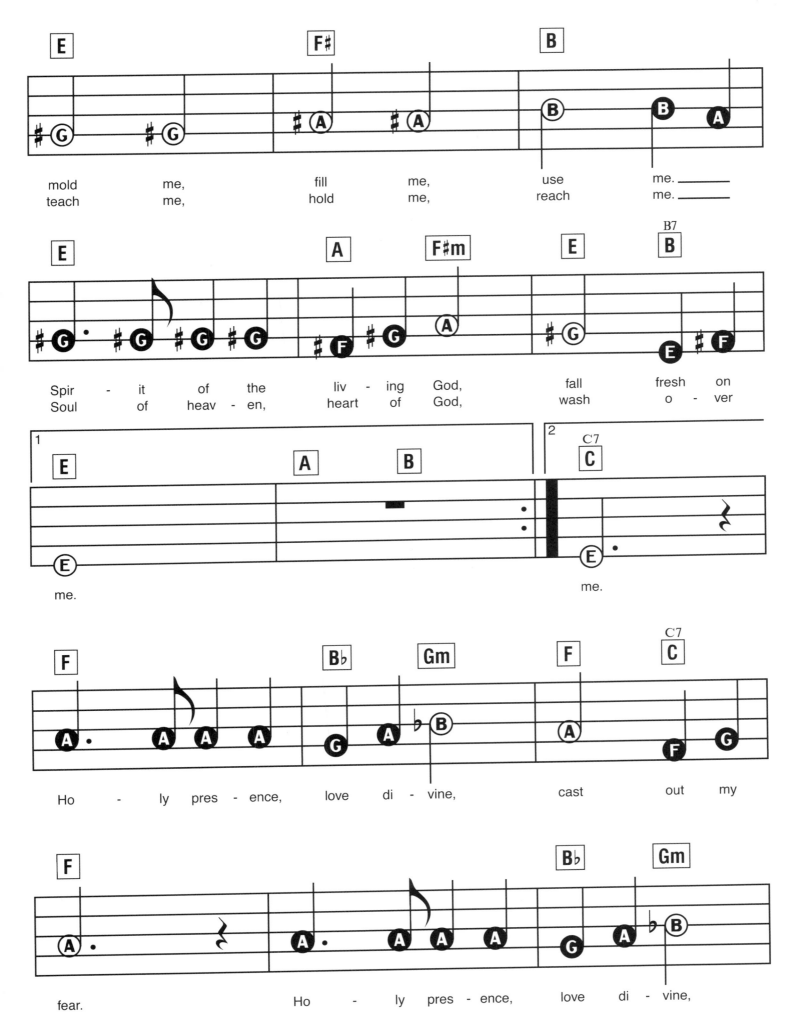

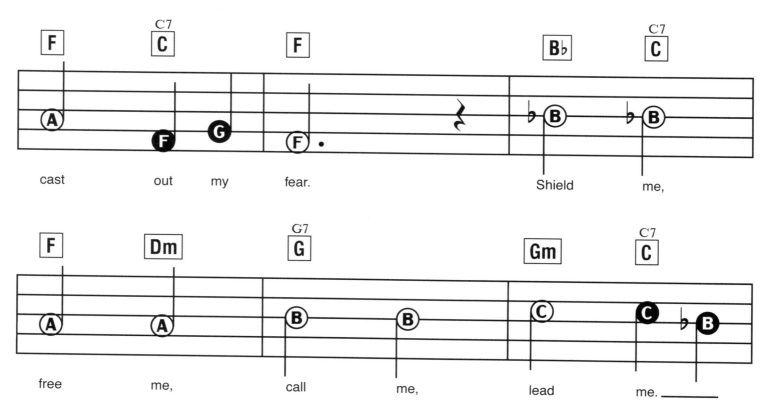

cast   out   my   fear.   Shield   me,

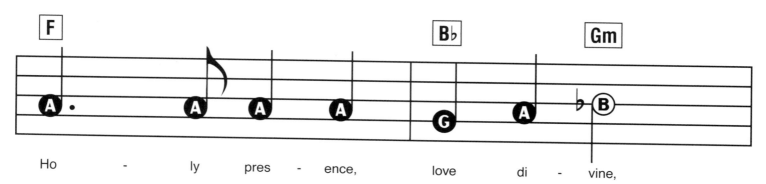

free   me,   call   me,   lead   me. _____

Ho   -   ly   pres - ence,   love   di   -   vine,

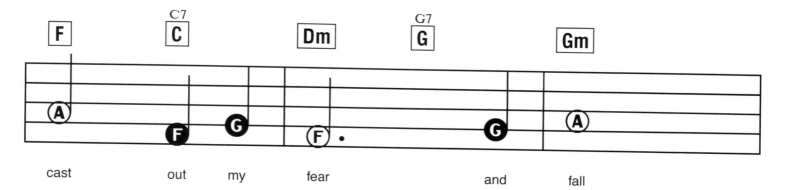

cast   out   my   fear   and   fall

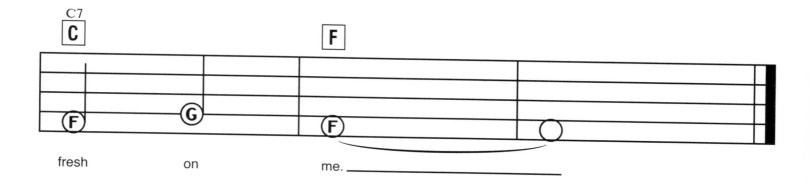

fresh   on   me. _____

Shout to the Lord

Registration 2
Rhythm: Ballad or 8-Beat

Words and Music by
Darlene Zschech

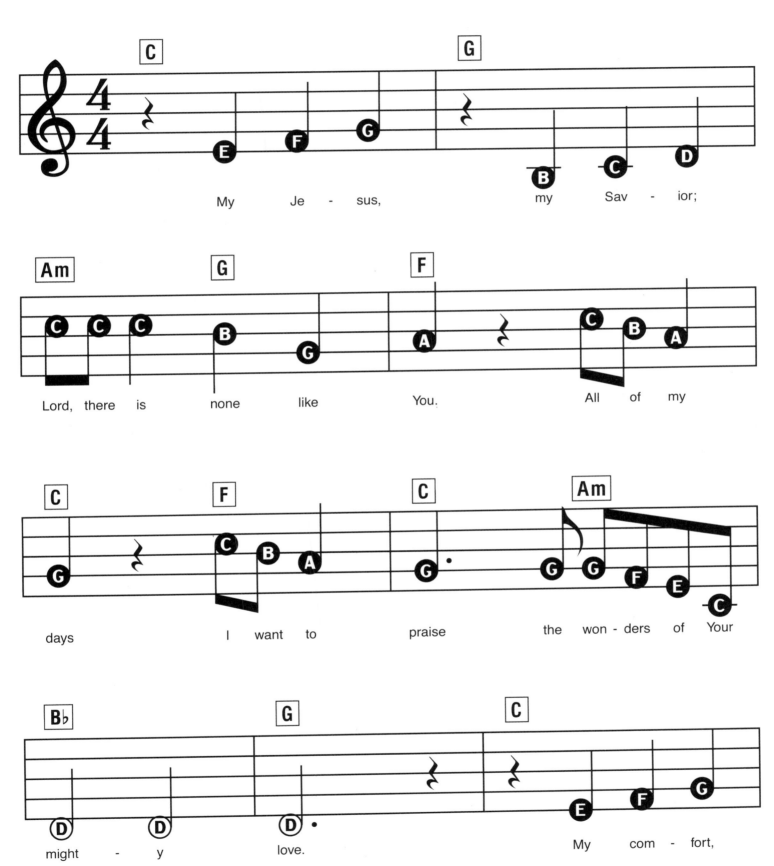

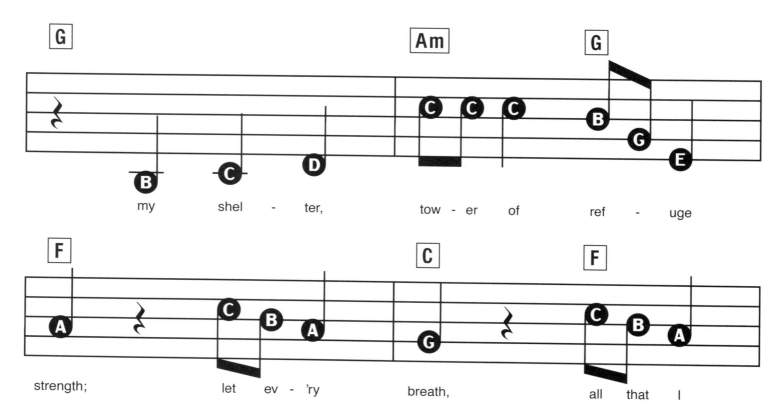

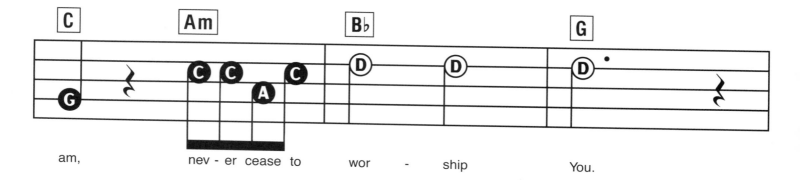

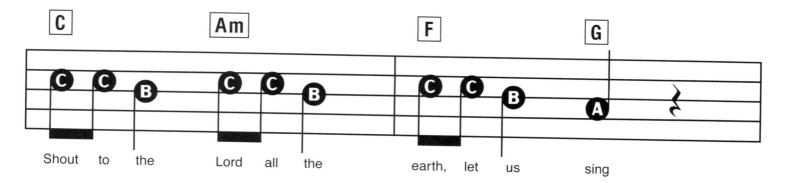

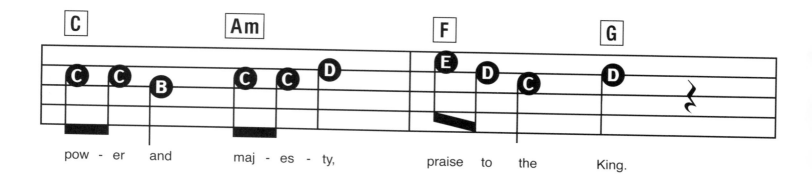

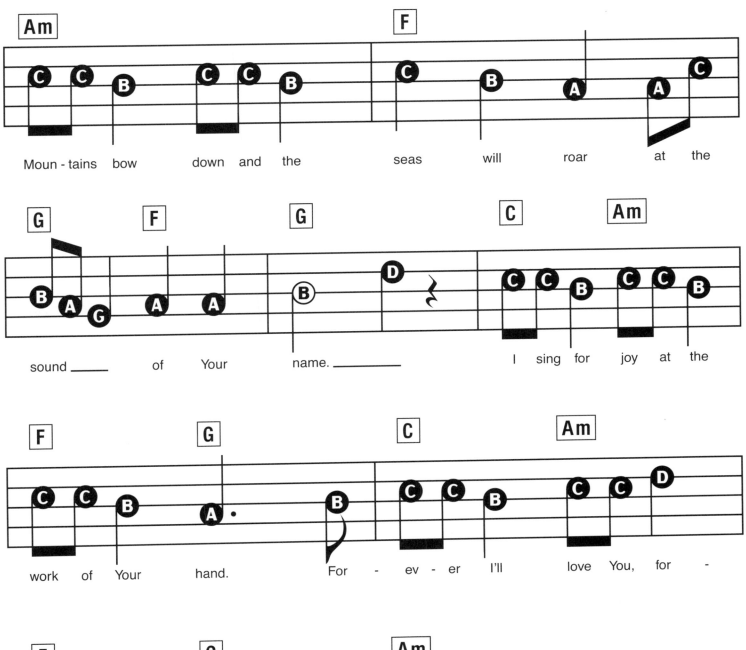

Moun - tains bow down and the seas will roar at the

sound ____ of Your name. ____ I sing for joy at the

work of Your hand. For - ev - er I'll love You, for -

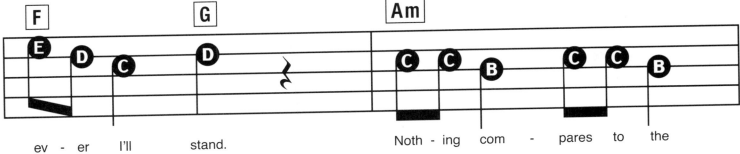

ev - er I'll stand. Noth - ing com - pares to the

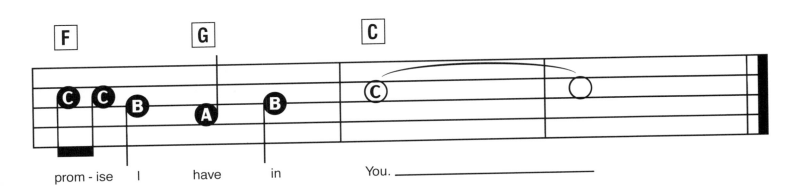

prom - ise I have in You. ____

Step by Step

Registration 4
Rhythm: 8-Beat or Ballad

Words and Music by
David Strasser "Beaker"

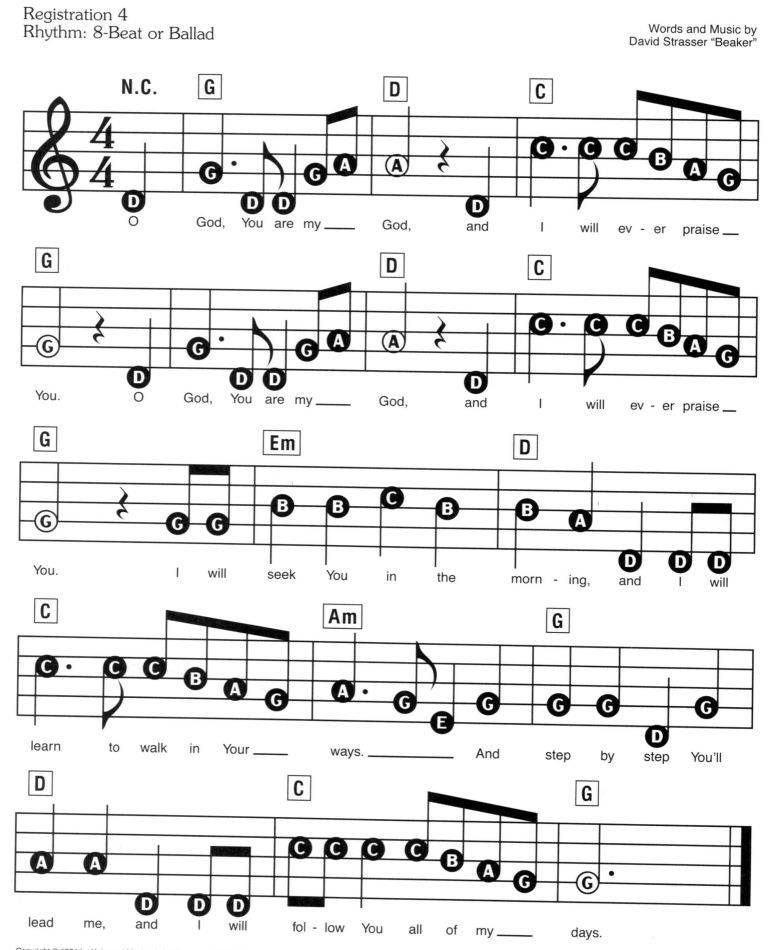

There Is None Like You

Registration 8
Rhythm: Ballad or 8-Beat

Words and Music by
Lenny LeBlanc

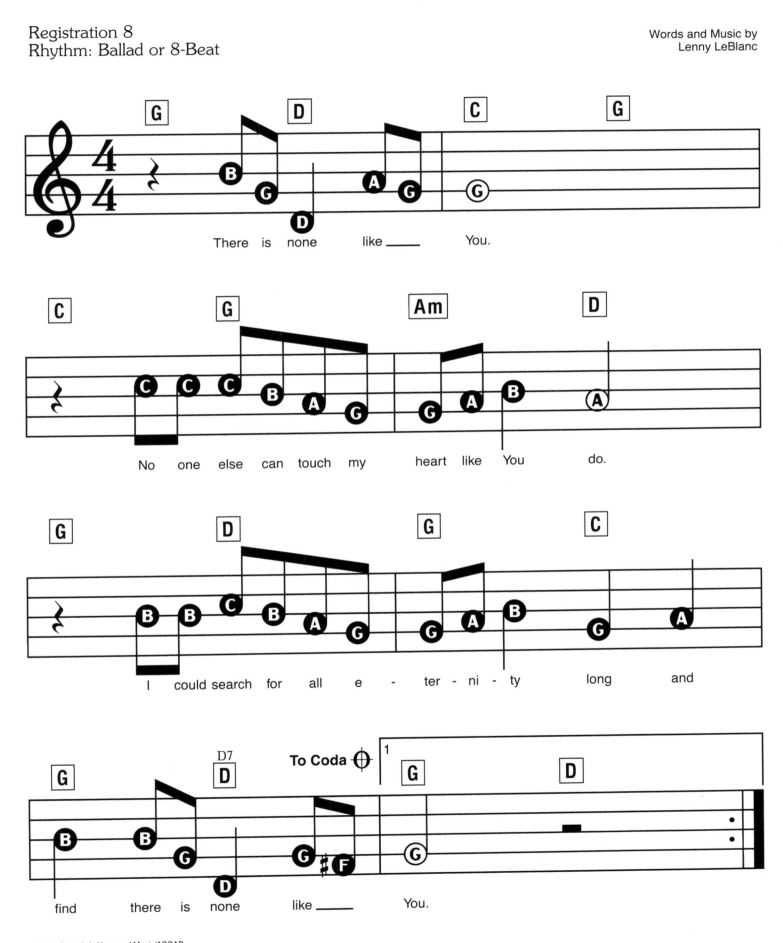

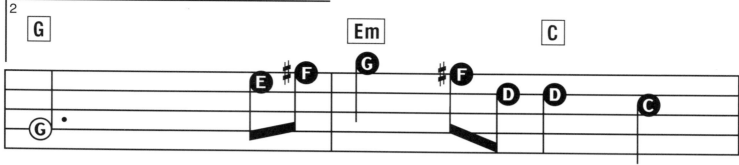

You.　　　　　　　　　(Instrumental)

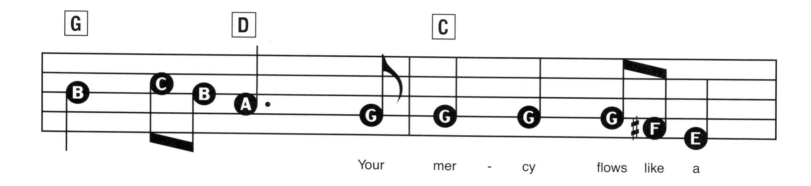

Your　mer - cy　flows　like　a

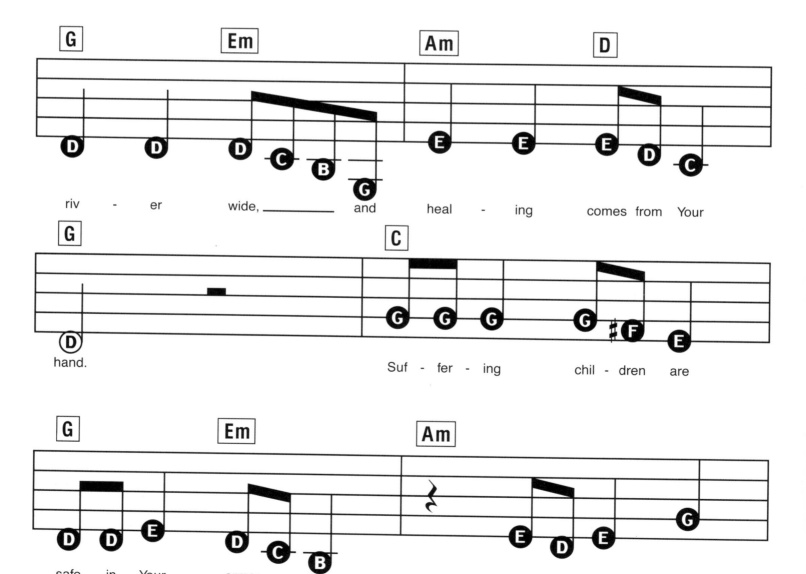

riv - er　wide, _____ and　heal - ing　comes　from　Your

hand.　　　　　　Suf - fer - ing　chil - dren　are

safe　in　Your　arms; _____　　　　　there　is　none　like

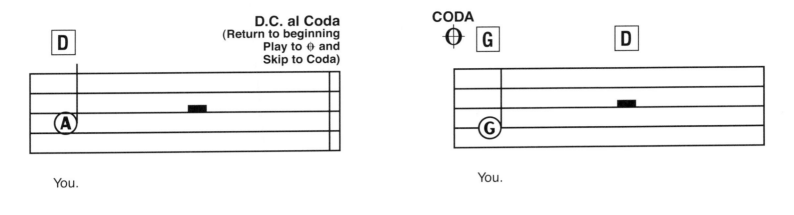

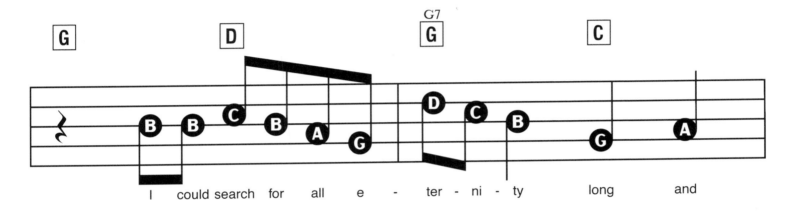

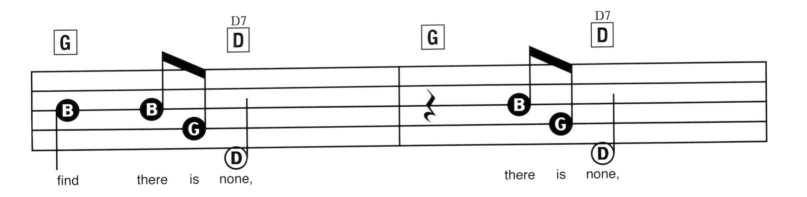

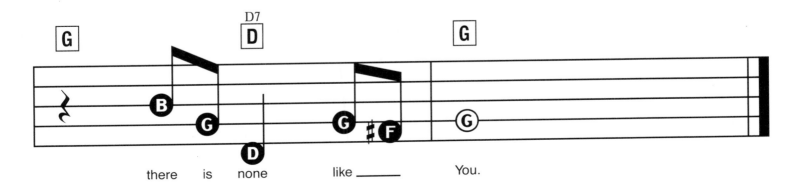

There Is a Redeemer

Registration 8
Rhythm: Ballad

Words and Music by
Melody Green

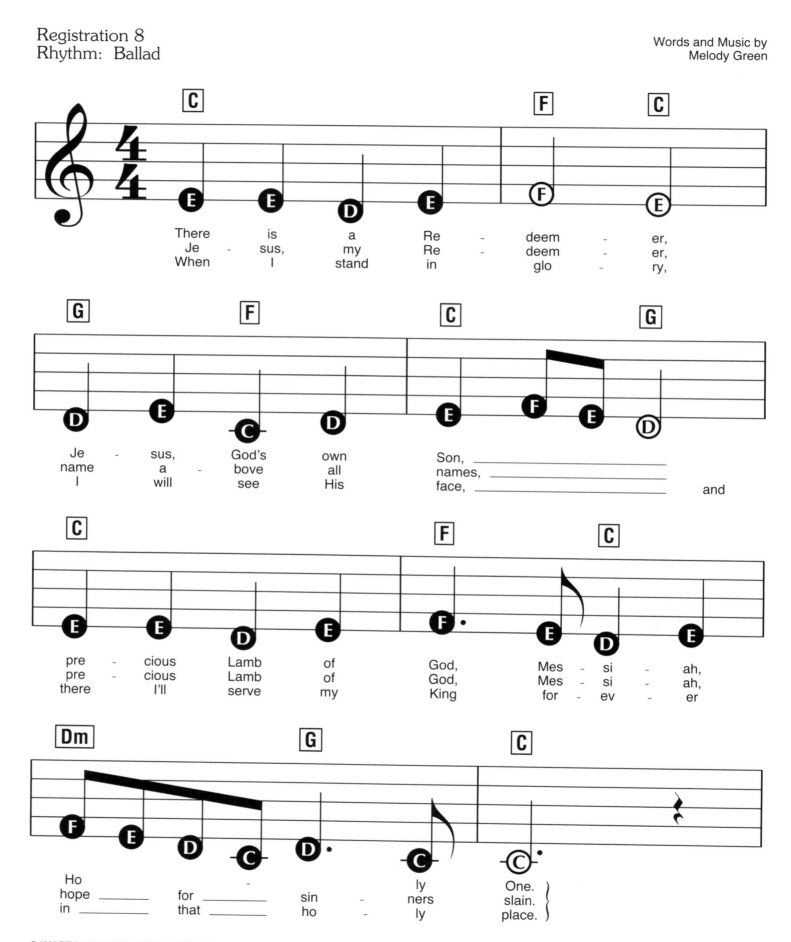

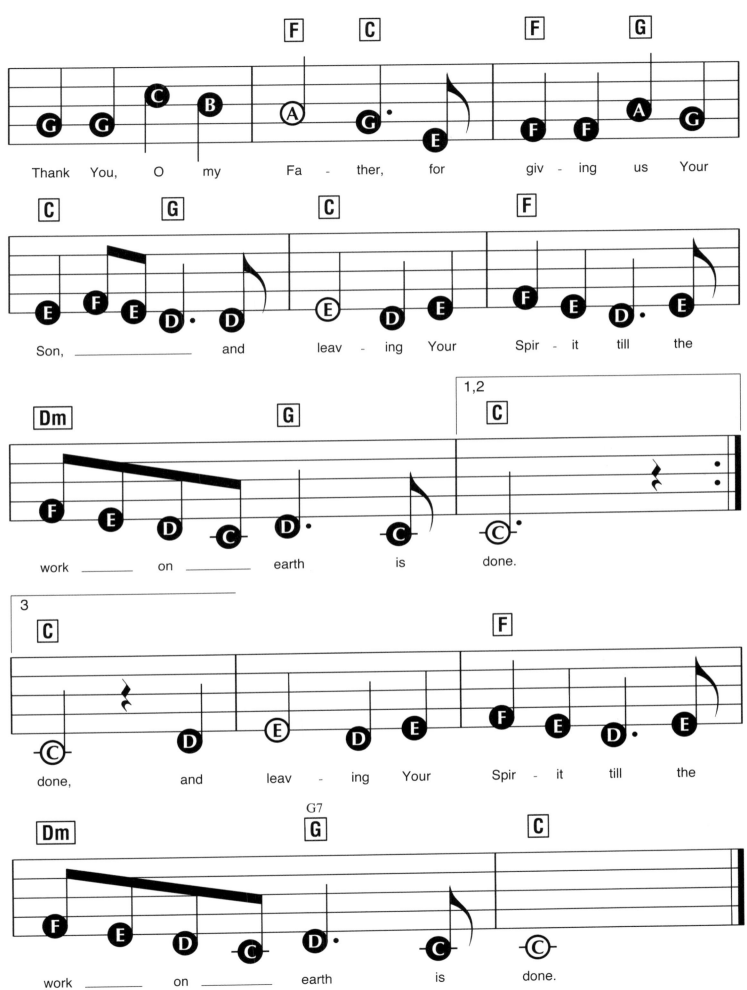

Thou Art Worthy

Registration 8
Rhythm: Waltz

Words and Music by
Pauline Michael Mills

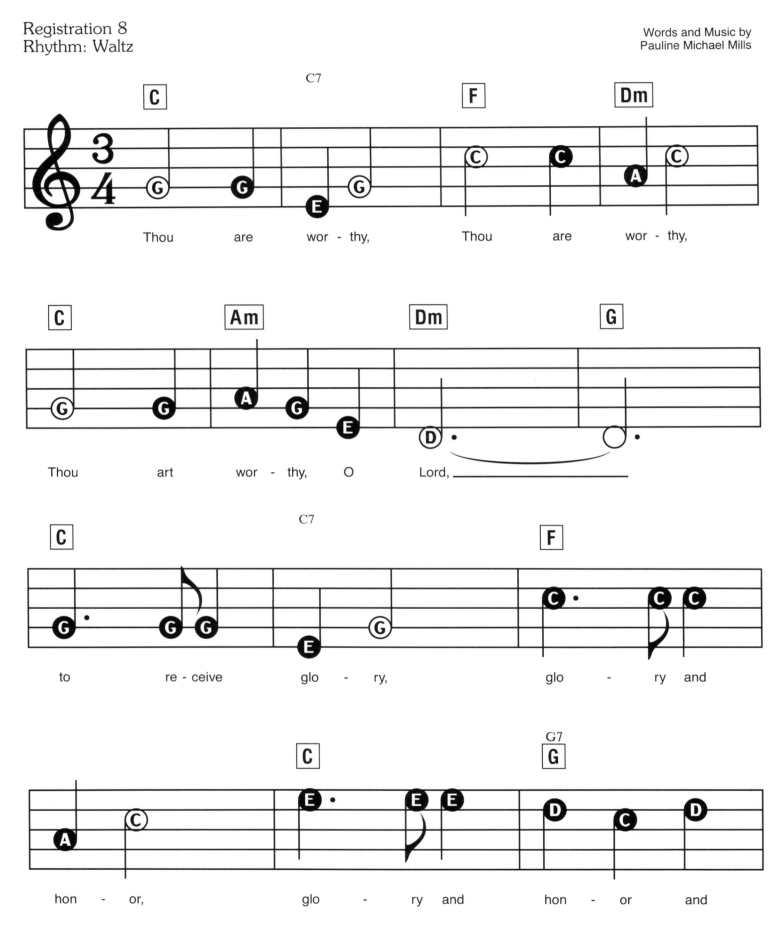

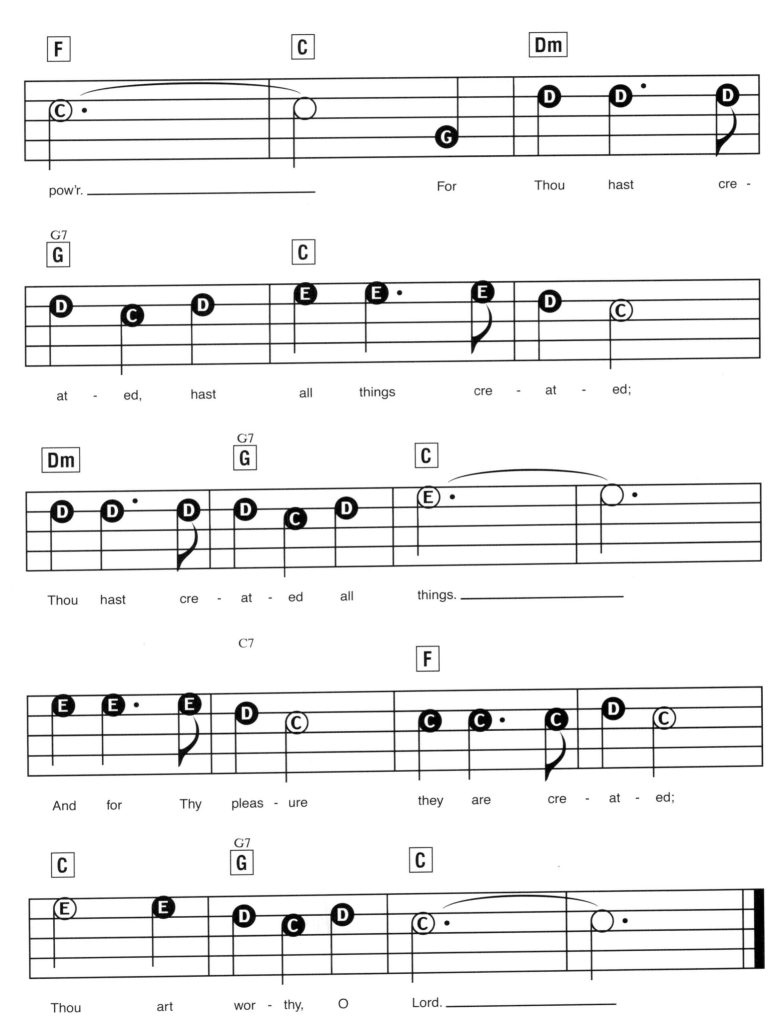

Victory Chant

Registration 5
Rhythm: African or 16-Beat

Words and Music by
Joseph Vogels

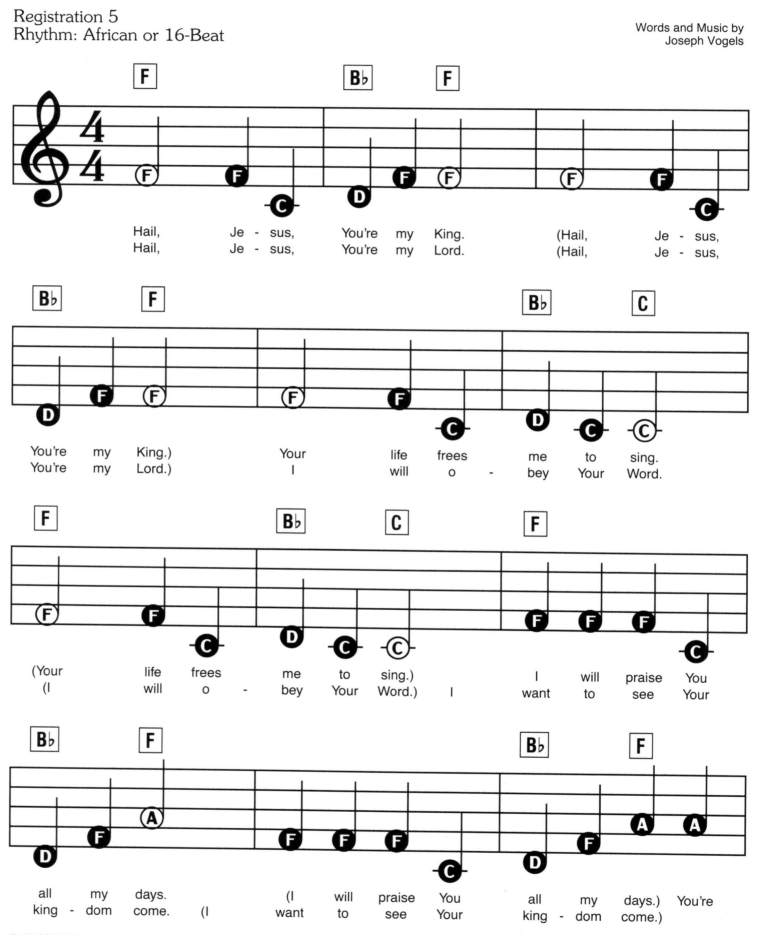

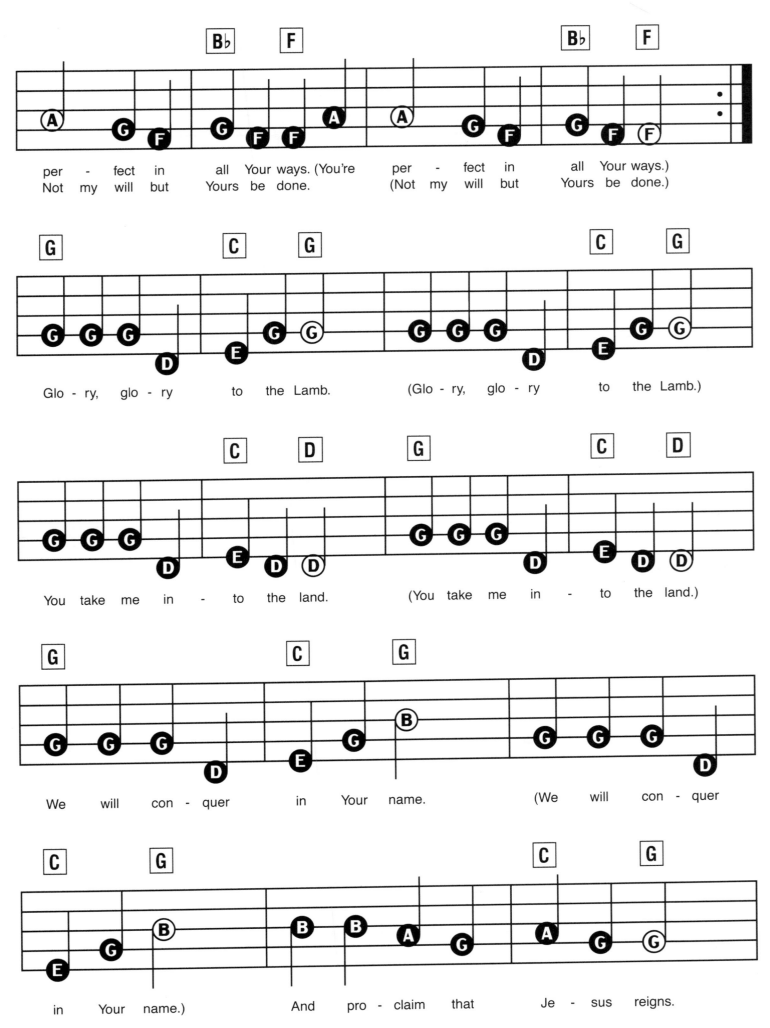

105

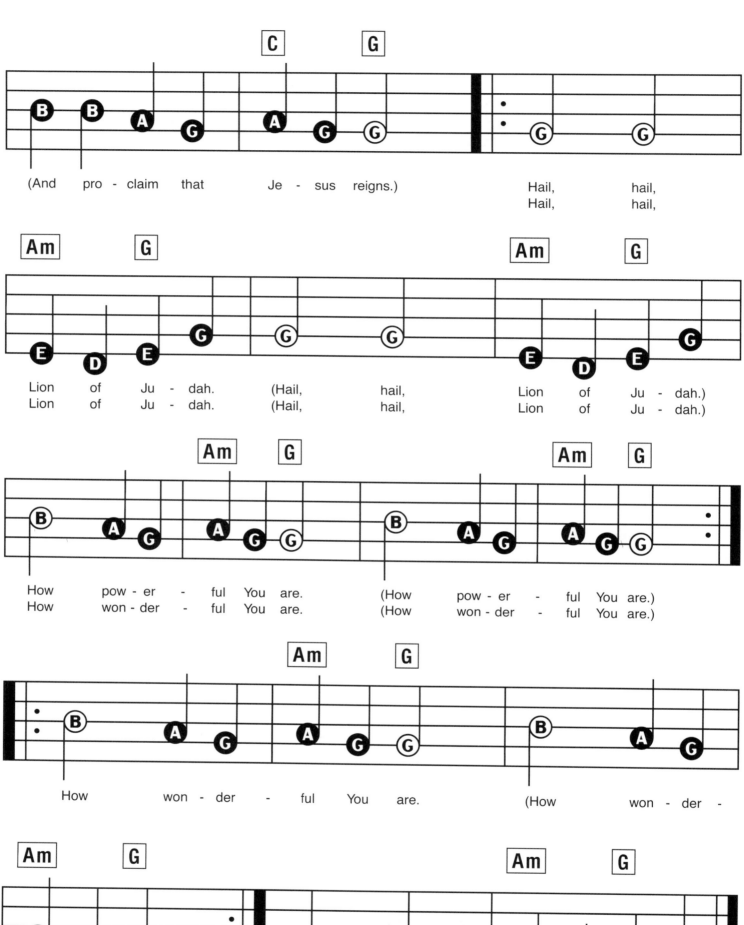

Worthy Is the Lamb

Registration 8
Rhythm: Ballad or 8-Beat

Words and Music by
Darlene Zschech

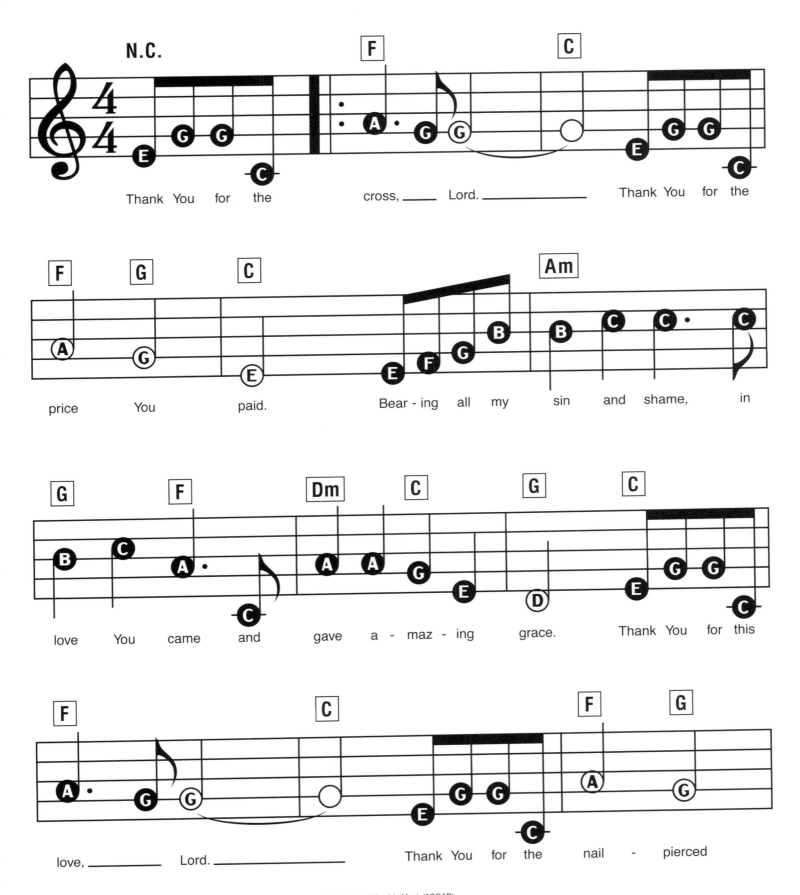

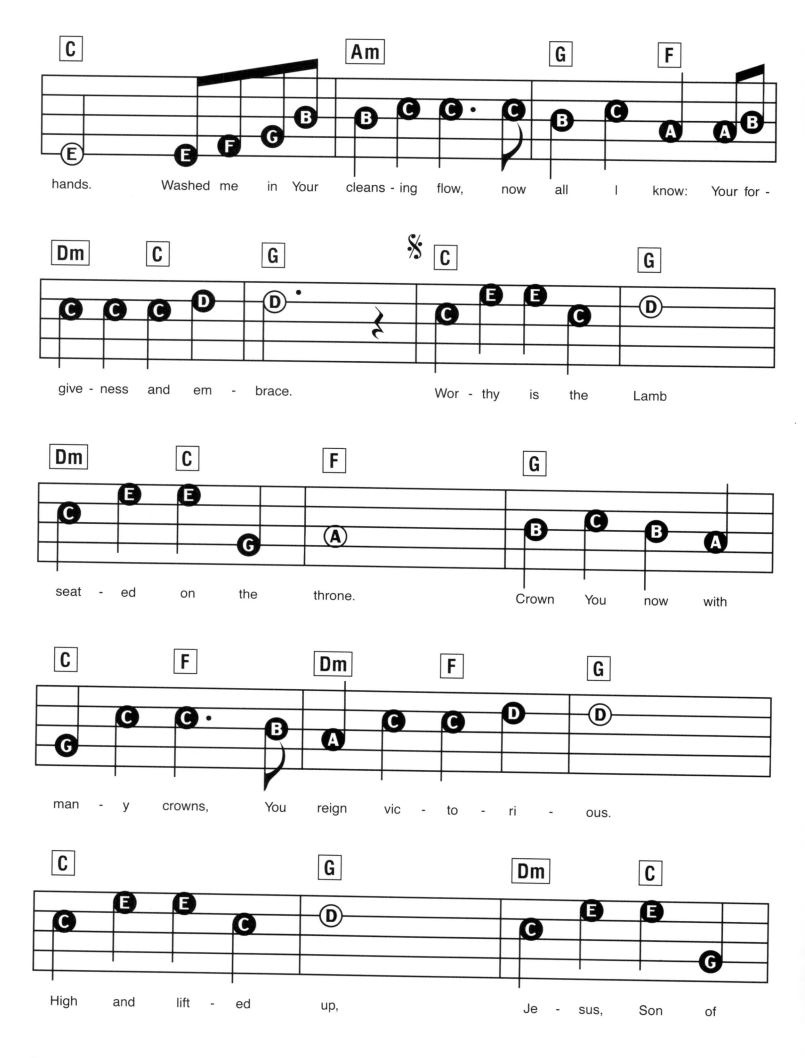

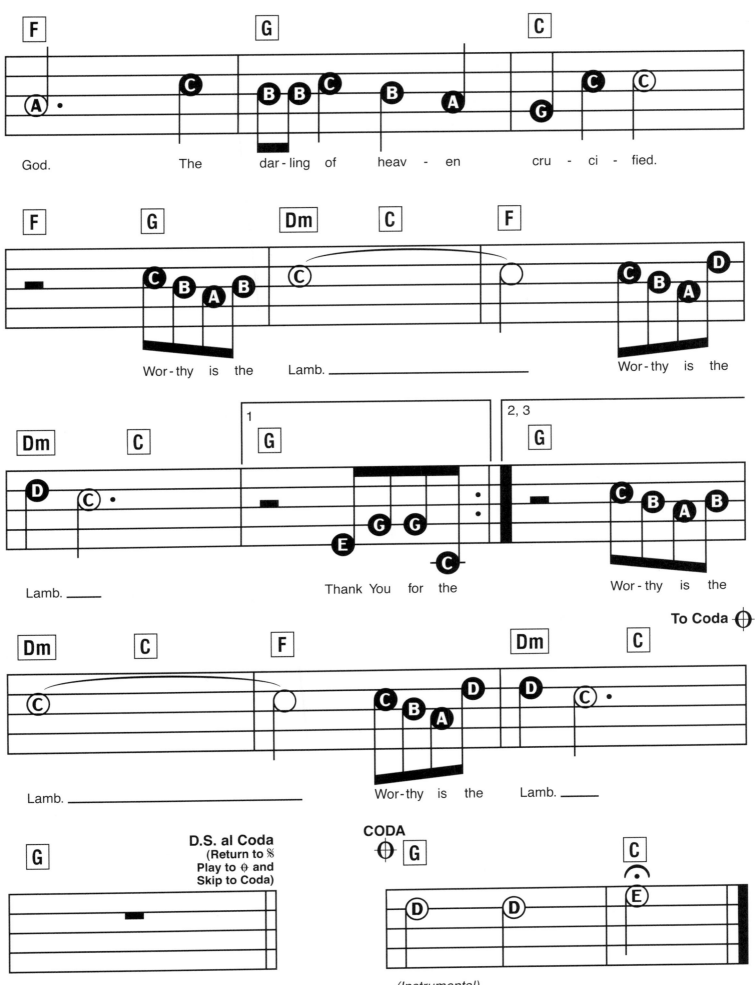

God. The dar-ling of heav-en cru-ci-fied.

Wor-thy is the Lamb. _____ Wor-thy is the

Lamb. _____ Thank You for the Wor-thy is the

To Coda ⊕

Lamb. _____ Wor-thy is the Lamb. _____

D.S. al Coda
(Return to 𝄋
Play to ⊕ and
Skip to Coda)

CODA
⊕

(Instrumental)

Worthy of Worship

Registration 2
Rhythm: Waltz

Words by Terry York
Music by Mark Blankenship

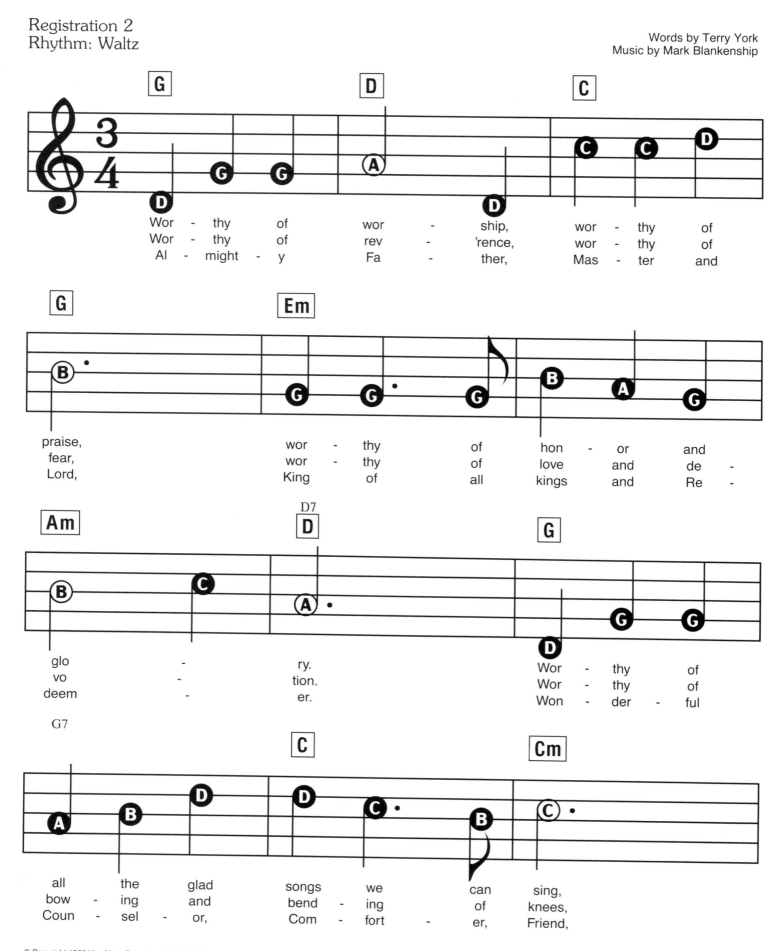

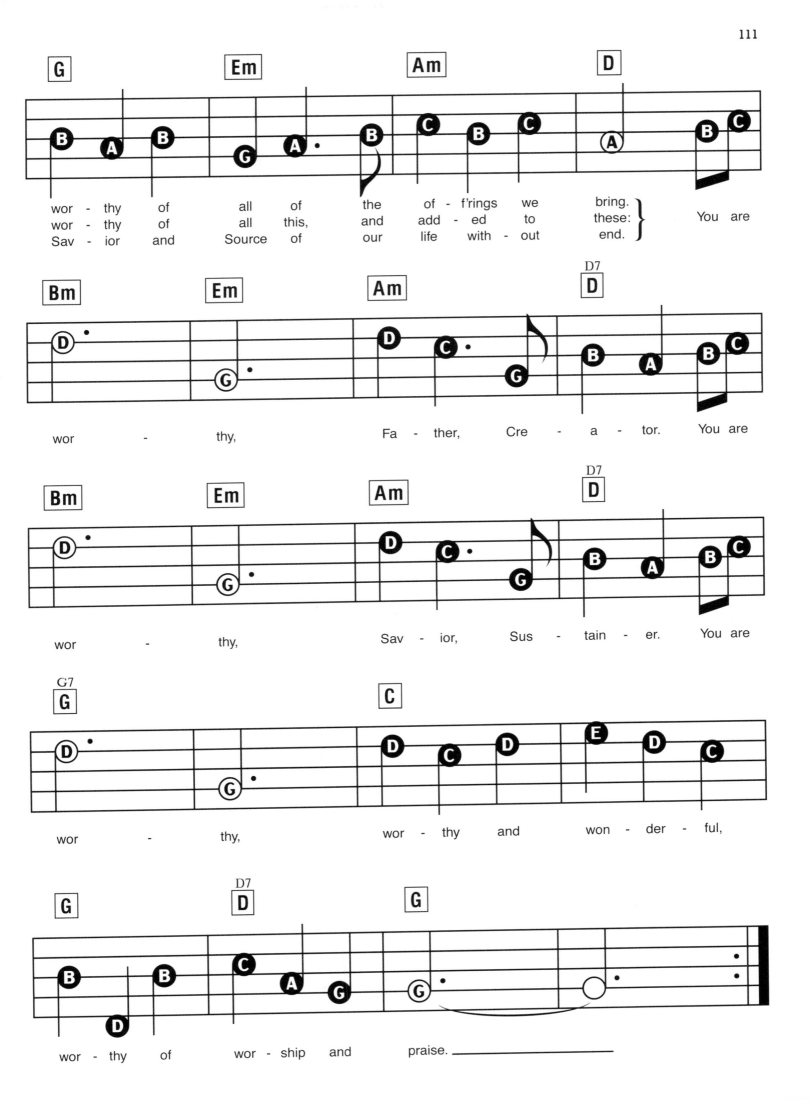

Worthy, You Are Worthy

Registration 1
Rhythm: Ballad

Words and Music by
Don Moen

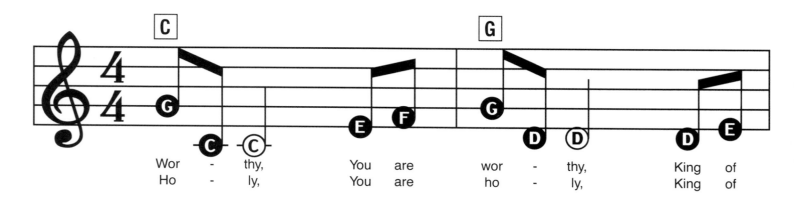

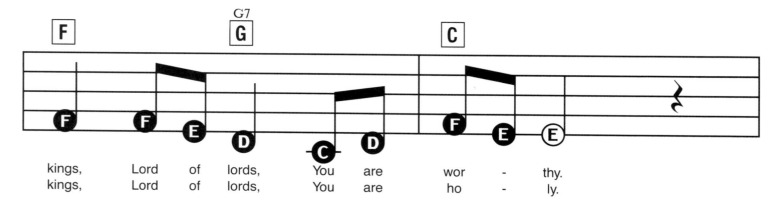

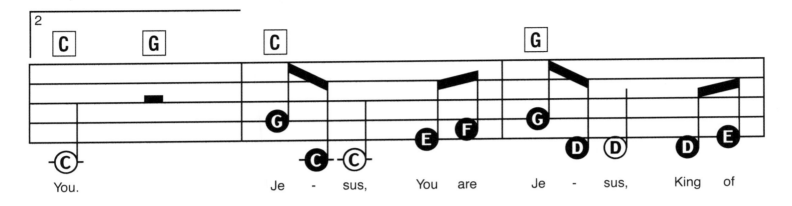

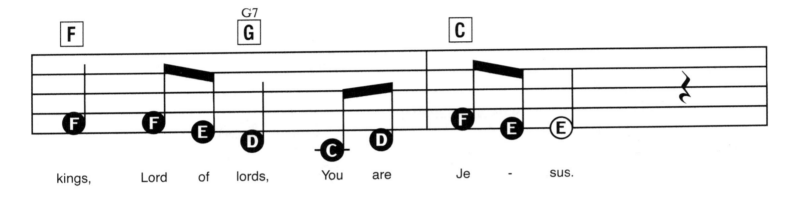

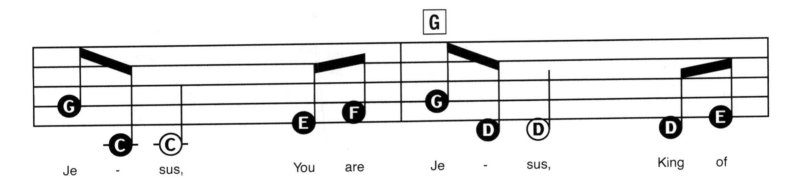

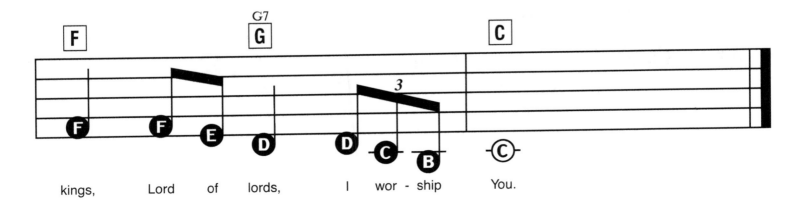

You Are My All in All

Registration 1
Rhythm: Ballad or 8-Beat

By Dennis Jernigan

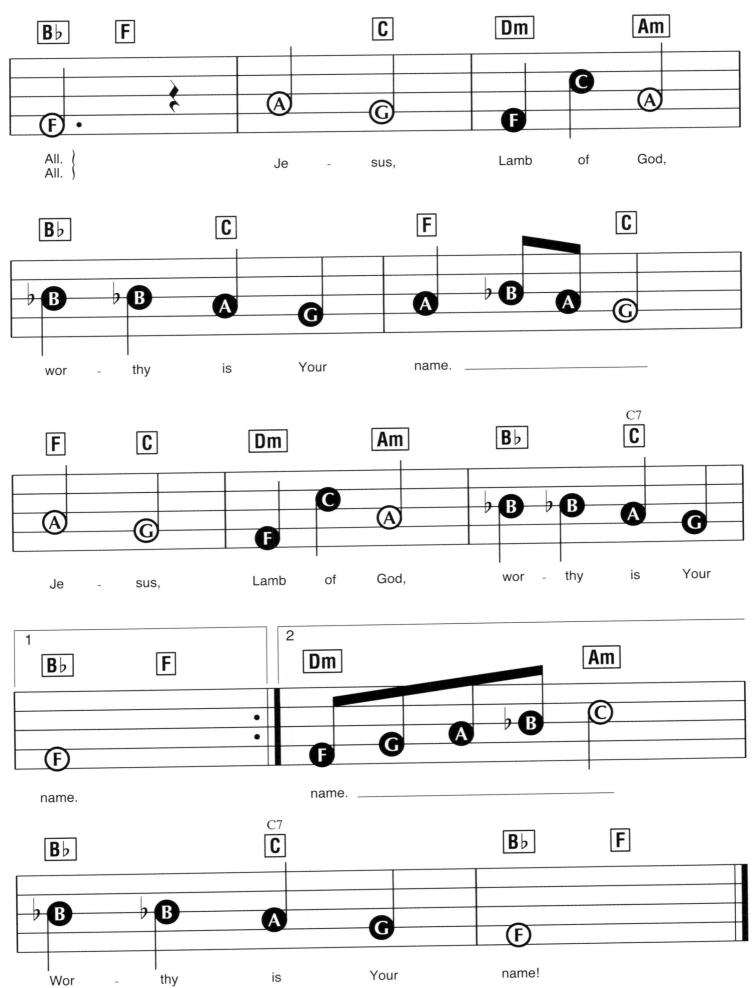

You're Worthy of My Praise

Registration 7
Rhythm: Pop or 8-Beat

Words and Music by
David Ruis

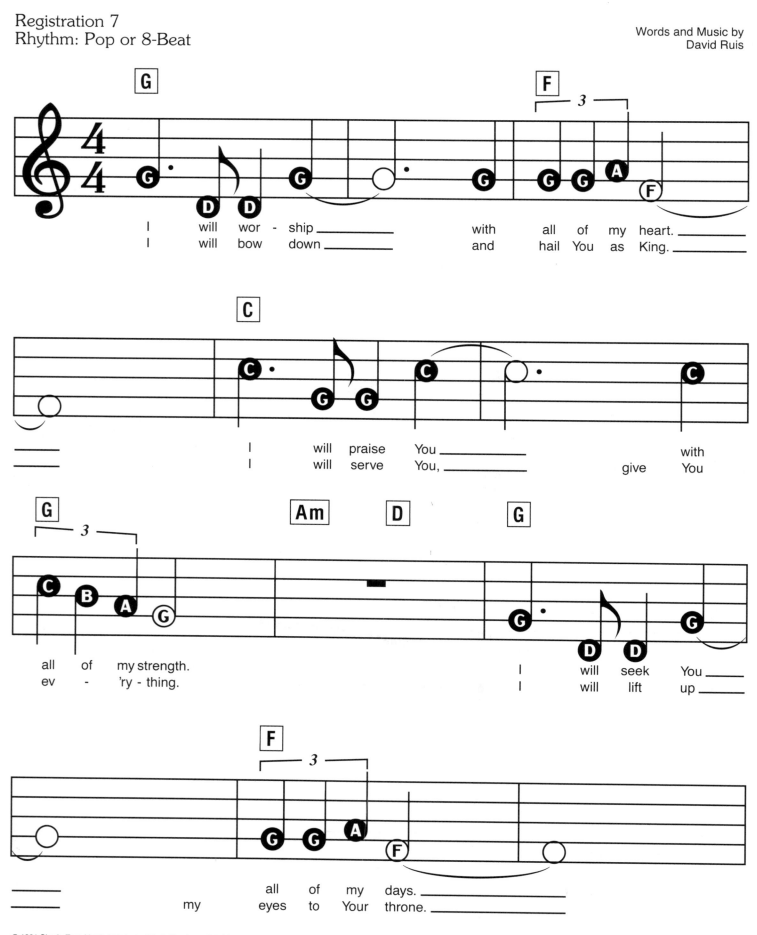

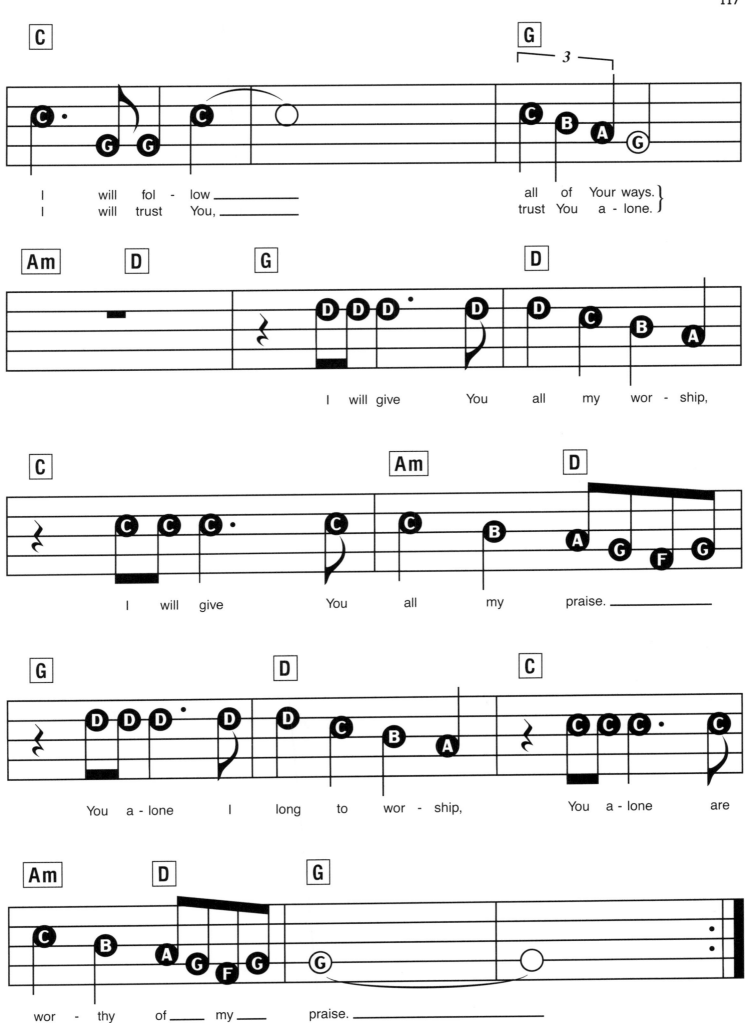

You Are My King
(Amazing Love)

Registration 8
Rhythm: Ballad or 8-Beat

Words and Music by
Billy James Foote

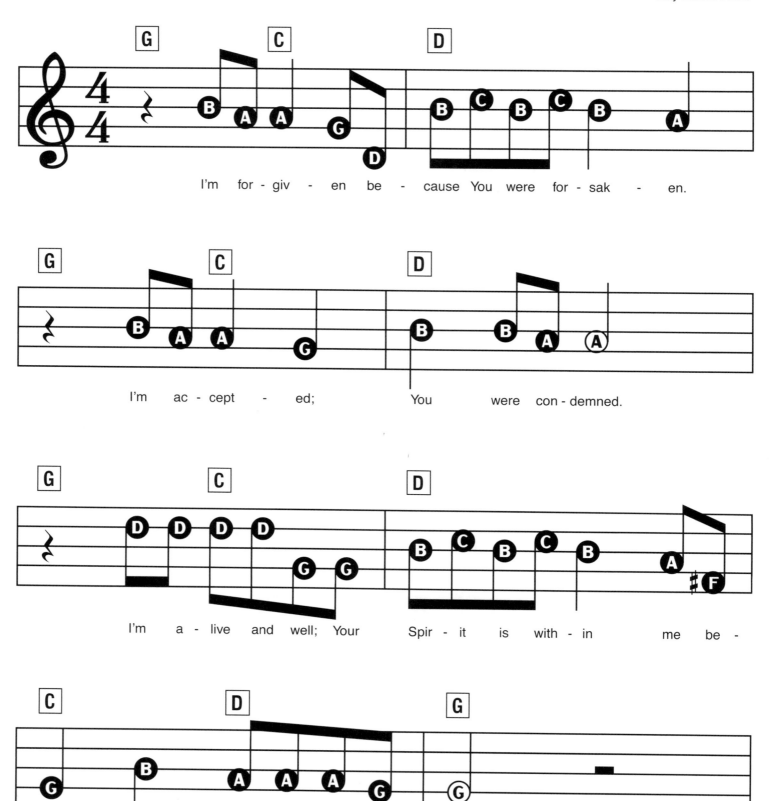

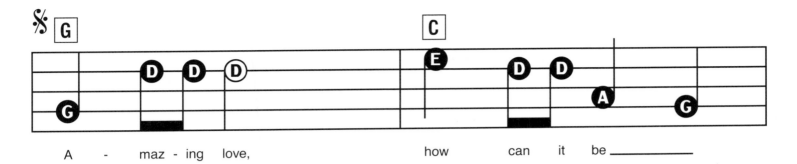

A - maz - ing love, how can it be _____

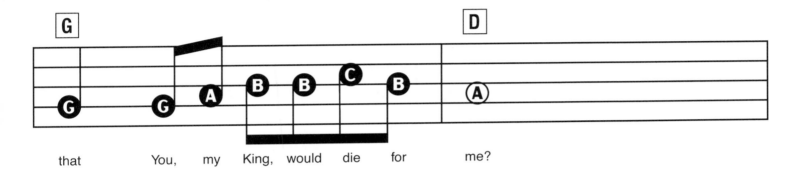

that You, my King, would die for me?

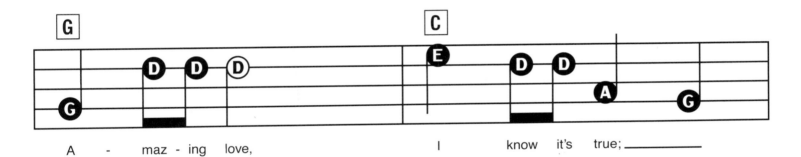

A - maz - ing love, I know it's true; _____

To Coda ⊕

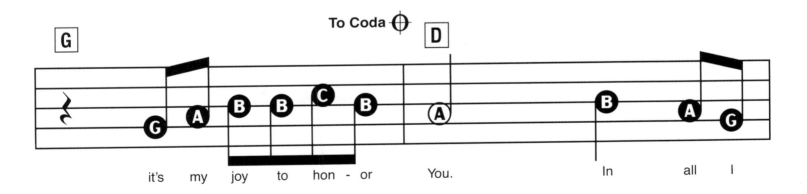

it's my joy to hon - or You. In all I

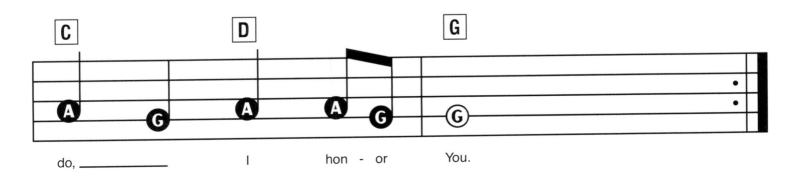

do, _____ I hon - or You.

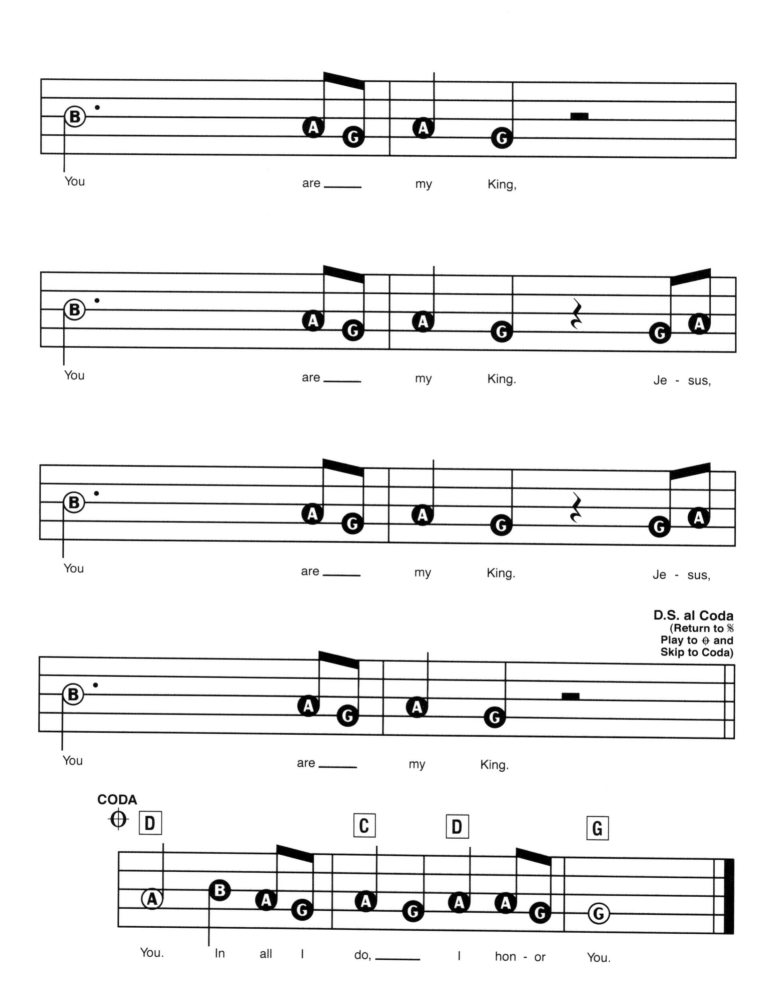